Unplugged Living: The Art and Science of Off-Grid Life

Creating Harmony with Nature and Independence

Megan Foster

Table of Contents

INTRODUCTION

Welcome to "Unplugged Living: The Art and Science of Off-Grid Life – Creating Harmony with Nature and Independence." Living off the grid has become popular as a revolutionary lifestyle option in a society where fast-paced living and digital connectedness rule. This book is an all-inclusive guide to living a life that respects the environment, encourages self-reliance, and honors the practice and philosophy of sustainable living.

In the pages that follow, we'll set out to investigate the essence of off-grid living—a way of life that defies convention and transcends the everyday expectations of modern life. Living off the grid is a conscious decision to reestablish a symbiotic rather than exploitative relationship with the natural world, not just a rejection of modern conveniences.

The off-grid lifestyle is dualistic, as the subtitle, "Creating Harmony with Nature and Independence," sums it up. On the one hand, we examine the scientific ideas behind sustainable systems, such as the use of renewable energy sources and the responsible management of waste and water resources. Conversely, we delve into the art of creating a life that melds harmoniously with the surroundings, promoting simplicity, mindfulness, and a stronger bond with the planet.

This book is not merely a guide; rather, it is an invitation to adopt a lifestyle that places a high value on ecological awareness, self-sufficiency, and a deep appreciation for the environment. "Unplugged Living" offers helpful advice, motivational tales, and a plethora of information to assist you in building a peaceful, self-sufficient, and sustainable life off the grid, regardless of whether you're thinking about making the switch or are just interested in learning more about the guiding principles of this way of life. Let's get exploring.

CHAPTER I

Understanding Off-Grid Living

What is Off-Grid Living?

Off-grid living represents a paradigm shift from conventional lifestyles, as individuals and communities choose to disconnect from centralized utilities and embrace self-sufficiency in meeting their essential needs. Off-grid living is a holistic approach that attempts to decrease dependency on external resources such as power, water, and sewage systems. At its foundation, off-grid living is living without relying on these resources. This way of living is a conscious decision to disengage from the trappings of contemporary conveniences to achieve a more sustainable and harmonious relationship with nature.

Off-grid living is characterized by the desire for energy independence, one of its distinguishing characteristics. There is a connection between traditional residences and centralized power networks, and these homes depend on electricity generated from fossil fuels. On the other hand, off-grid residents power their homes using alternative and renewable energy sources they have developed themselves. Solar panels, wind turbines, and hydroelectric systems are typical installations that convert the energy of the sun, wind, and flowing water into electricity that may be used. This shift toward decentralized energy generation lessens the environmental impact and encourages a sense of autonomy by allowing individuals to create their power.

Another essential component of off-grid living is providing one's water supply. Rainwater harvesting systems, well water extraction, and other effective water management measures are implemented by off-grinders so that they do not have to rely on municipal water sources. In addition to providing a reliable water source, rainwater collection and storage raises awareness about the importance of water conservation and provides a sustainable water source. Off-grid communities frequently use natural filtering techniques when it comes to water purification. This allows them to maintain a clean and dependable water supply without centralized water treatment facilities.

Living off the grid encompasses the management of electricity and water and the management of trash sustainably. To reduce their environmental impact, those who live off the grid embrace environmentally friendly behaviors. These actions typically include recycling and composting toilets. Individuals learn to repurpose and recycle items, which helps to promote a mindset of environmental stewardship. Waste reduction becomes a priority, and individuals learn to recycle materials. By assuming responsibility for their garbage, those who live off the grid contribute to conserving natural ecosystems and reduce the demand placed on public waste disposal systems.

The conscious design of homes and living spaces brings them into harmony with the natural environment and is the source of the creativity that is off-grid living. Architecture in off-grid communities frequently emphasizes the use of environmentally friendly construction materials, designs that are energy efficient, and structural integration with the natural environment. Creating structures that are indistinguishable from their natural surroundings lessens the impact on the environment and improves the whole experience of living off the grid. Gardening, implementing permaculture principles, and creating outdoor areas that encourage a connection with the Earth and nurture a profound respect for the natural world are all activities that can be done by those who live off the grid.

A fundamental adjustment in thinking toward simplicity and mindfulness is also required to decide to live an off-grid existence. People who live off the grid frequently adopt a minimalist lifestyle, emphasizing quality over quantity and placing a higher value on experiences than material goods. Individuals are encouraged to reconsider their priorities due to this deliberate transition away from consumer-driven cultures, resulting in a stronger sense of fulfillment and contentment. Pursuing a simpler life is not about deprivation; instead, it is about making a deliberate decision to concentrate on what is genuinely essential, which aligns with the ideals of sustainability and self-sufficiency.

This way of life has a significant psychological and emotional component, even though the practical features of off-grid living are readily apparent in implementing environmentally friendly practices and sustainable technologies. People who live off the grid frequently report feeling a stronger connection to the natural environment, which can positively impact their mental health and give them a sense of purpose in life. Off-grid areas provide individuals with the opportunity to reconnect with themselves, which in turn fosters reflection and personal development. These locations are characterized by their solitude and calm. In this particular facet of off-grid life, the profound relationship between the exterior environment and one's internal well-being is brought to light.

Being resilient, adaptable, and having a strong sense of community are all necessary qualities for navigating the problems of living off the grid. Those who live off the grid may have to contend with several logistical challenges, including acquiring supplies, managing adverse weather conditions, and resolving unforeseen maintenance concerns. Nevertheless, these obstacles are overcome by a spirit of self-reliance and a network of people who support one another and share similar values. Creating a flourishing and resilient collective is a common goal of off-grid communities, which frequently prioritize collaboration and sharing knowledge, resources, and experiences.

Off-grid life requires individuals to have several important considerations, one of which is financial independence. The initial investment in environmentally friendly technology and infrastructure may be substantial; nevertheless, the long-term savings and decreased reliance on various outside services will help achieve financial independence. Individuals who live off the grid frequently investigate other sources of income, such as working from home, engaging in sustainable agriculture, or engaging in artisanal efforts. This allows them to connect their economic activities with their ideals of autonomy and sustainability. Not only does this financial self-sufficiency promote the viability of living off the grid, but it also offers a model for an economic system that is more resilient and decentralized.

Because the off-grid movement is continuing to gain steam, it is essential to recognize the variety within this way of living. Living off the grid is not a one-size-fits-all method; instead, it comprises a spectrum of options and modifications that may be tailored to the preferences and circumstances of each individual. There is a wide range of distinctions between off-grid communities regarding their structures and ideas, ranging from eco-villages with shared resources to secluded lodges in the wilderness. These differences are a reflection of the freedom that is inherent in off-grid living, which enables individuals to personalize their experience so that it is in line with their specific values and objectives.

The conclusion is that living off the grid is a deliberate break from traditional ways of life and provides a way to achieve better sustainability, self-sufficiency, and harmony with nature. The art and science of off-grid living encompasses a holistic approach that includes the utilization of renewable energy sources, the attainment of water self-sufficiency, the adoption of sustainable waste management, the design of environmentally friendly homes, the cultivation of a conscious attitude, and the promotion of a feeling of community. While exploring the possibilities of living off the grid, individuals and communities contribute not only to their own personal well-being but also to the more significant movement toward a more resilient, environmentally sensitive, and peaceful way of life.

Benefits and Challenges

The 21st century has undeniably become the era of unprecedented technological advancements, marking a transformative shift in how we live, work, and interact. Innovation has left an indelible effect on practically every aspect of human existence, from the rise of the internet to the spread of smartphones. The terrain of innovation has been extensive and varied, giving rise to a wide range of innovations. This section investigates technology's impact on various aspects of society, including communication, healthcare, education, and business. It looks into the myriad of facets comprising the benefits and challenges linked with the widespread adoption of technology.

A significant force that has evolved in the area of communication is technology, which reduces the world's massive expanse into a global village-sized community. The introduction of the internet and the following mushrooming of social media platforms have fundamentally altered how humans engage with one another and exchange information. A sense of connectivity has been fostered due to the instantaneous nature of communication, enabling it to transcend geographical barriers. In business, technologies that will allow video conferencing have become vital tools because they make it possible to collaborate seamlessly across multiple time zones and continents. This interconnectedness has made it easier to form personal ties and prompted global collaboration on a scale that was inconceivable just a few decades ago.

Technology improvements have been the driving force behind a transformation that has taken place in the healthcare industry. Combining cutting-edge medical technology and artificial intelligence (AI) has increased diagnosis accuracy and treatment effectiveness. The emerging field of telemedicine has the potential to revolutionize the healthcare industry by enabling remote access to medical treatments and easing the burden placed on physical institutions. A move toward preventative healthcare is being fostered by the proliferation of wearable devices and health-tracking applications, which allow consumers to monitor their health proactively. Not only has the combined use of technology and healthcare led to better outcomes for patients, but it has also ushered in a new era of customized medicine, which involves tailoring therapies to the specific genetic profiles of each patient.

Additionally, incorporating technology has resulted in a transformation of the educational system overall. Through online learning platforms, education has become more accessible to more people, removing obstacles based on geography and socioeconomic status. Students from all over the world have access to classes offered by major educational institutions, which paves the way for a learning environment that is more varied and inclusive. Traditional methods of instruction have been revolutionized by the introduction of interactive technology, such as virtual reality, which has turned complex topics into more exciting and understandable issues. Not only has the digitization of education made it more accessible, but it has also made it possible to pursue learning throughout one's life. This has ensured that education is a pursuit that continues throughout one's entire life rather than a phase that comes to an end.

Technology has been a driving force behind change in the corporate world, helping to cultivate creativity and reversing the paradigms established in the past. Across a wide range of industries, automation, driven by robotics and artificial intelligence, has resulted in streamlined processes, leading to higher efficiency and cost savings. As a result of its ability to provide organizations with real-time insights into customer behavior and industry trends, data analytics has evolved as a fundamental component of strategic decision- making. E-commerce platforms have brought about a revolution in the retail industry by providing customers with an unprecedented level of convenience and giving businesses access to a worldwide market. Not only has the incorporation of technology into business processes been a driving force behind the expansion of the economy, but it has also been a catalyst for the development of new business models and industries.

Nevertheless, despite these tremendous advantages, the mass adoption of technology is more than just tricky. Among the most critical worries is the effect that it will have on employment. As a result of the displacement of specific jobs brought about by automation and artificial intelligence, serious issues have been raised regarding the future of employment. It is necessary for there to be a matching evolution in the skills and abilities that are required in the workforce to accommodate the rapid evolution of technology. Policymakers, industries, and educational institutions must work together to address the tremendous task of finding a way to strike a careful balance between advancing technology and maintaining employment prospects.

In the wake of technology improvements, the digital divide is one of the most notable challenges that has emerged. However, subsets of the population need access to these revolutionary tools even though technology has made unlimited potential available to many. The digital divide, both within and across countries, exacerbates pre-existing disparities and makes it more challenging to move up the socioeconomic ladder. To bridge this gap, it is necessary to ensure that technology becomes a force that equalizes rather than a source of division. This will ensure that the advantages of innovation are accessible to all individuals, regardless of their socioeconomic level or geographical location.

The age of pervasive technology has also given rise to worries over privacy and security, which have become critical issues. Questions regarding preserving individuals' privacy are raised due to the collecting, storing, and analyzing enormous volumes of personal data. The necessity of implementing stringent cybersecurity measures has been brought to light by high-profile data breaches and incidences of unauthorized access. It is a challenging endeavor that involves the development of extensive legal and ethical frameworks to achieve the delicate balance that must be struck between innovation and the protection of human privacy.

The rapid pace of technological advancement also presents difficulties regarding the regulatory frameworks and ethical issues that must be considered. The rapid advancement of technology frequently causes legislation to need help to keep up with technological advancement, which results in governance and accountability gaps. To ensure that technological breakthroughs are by social values and ethical standards, it is necessary to have deliberate and thorough frameworks. Ethical considerations, such as the responsible use of artificial intelligence and biotechnology, call for such frameworks. The obligation falls not only with legislators but also with engineers, corporations, and the greater society to collectively manage the ethical consequences of technological progress.

When it comes to the trajectory of human progress, the benefits and obstacles of adopting technical advancements in the 21st century weave a complicated tapestry that affects the trajectory of human progress. It is impossible to deny the tremendous influence that this has had on communication, healthcare, education, and business, bringing in opportunities and efficiency that have never been seen before. Nevertheless, the difficulties associated with employment, the digital divide, privacy concerns, and ethical considerations are equally significant and call for solutions to be developed carefully. As society continues to navigate the complex landscape of technological breakthroughs, it will be essential to take an approach that is collaborative, adaptable, and morally mindful to shape a future in which technology serves as a force for positive change, which will be to the advantage of humanity as a whole.

Types of Off-Grid Lifestyles

The concept of living off-grid, detached from conventional utilities and infrastructure, has gained traction in recent years, reflecting a growing desire for independence and sustainability. Off-grid lives are as varied as the people who choose to adopt them. These lifestyles can range from living in lonely huts in the wilderness to residing in sustainable communities that encourage an attitude of self-sufficiency. This section explores the many different kinds of off-grid living, focusing on the distinctive qualities and difficulties linked with each lifestyle.

The isolated wilderness cabin dweller lifestyle is often considered to be one of the most iconic off-grid lifestyles. These individuals, who live in the depths of forests or perched on the shores of distant lakes, opt for a life of solitude and self-sufficiency rather than the amenities that come with living in an urban environment. They construct their cabins using materials that are acquired from the surrounding area, they generate electricity through the use of solar panels or wind turbines, and they rely on rainwater collection or well water. The attractiveness of this way of living lies in the fact that it allows one to live in peace with nature, fostering a deep connection with the environment and giving one a sense of autonomy; yet, it also comes with a number of problems, including extremely harsh weather conditions, restricted access to supplies, and the requirement of substantial survival skills.

Another off-grid lifestyle gaining popularity is the homesteader lifestyle, typically portrayed as an individual cultivating a plot of land, growing their food, and raising their livestock. To achieve self-sufficiency, homesteaders often follow a hybrid approach incorporating traditional and contemporary methods. They might use the ideas of permaculture, engage in regenerative agriculture, and use renewable energy sources to reduce their negative impact on the environment. The homesteading lifestyle requires hard work, devotion, and a steep learning curve to acquire various skills, ranging from agriculture to animal husbandry. However, it offers a sense of connection to the land and the satisfaction of providing one's nutrition.

Communities that are not connected to the grid are an additional aspect of this way of life, which places an emphasis on communal self-sufficiency and the sharing of resources. Eco-villages and communal farms are two examples of the great variety of intentional communities that may be found all over the world. Residents frequently work together to develop sustainable living habits, participating in the distribution of tasks such as the production of food, the management of waste, and the creation of energy. The common principles of environmental stewardship, cooperation, and a desire to decreasing their ecological footprint are what make off-grid communities appealing to people who are interested in living independently. The success of such communities, on the other hand, is contingent upon productive communication, the development of consensus, and the existence of a common vision among their members. The sense of community and belonging in these off-grid lifestyles is a powerful draw for many.

"modern nomad" refers to a lifestyle distinct from other off-grid lifestyles. A dependency on portable electronics and continual mobility between different areas defines this lifestyle. Digital nomads, for example, take advantage of the possibility of working remotely to allow themselves to maintain a lifestyle that involves regular travel and exploration. Mobile homes, such as recreational vehicles (RVs) or vans that have been transformed into homes, are frequently chosen by them. These homes are typically outfitted with solar panels and composting toilets. An individual can work and live according to their terms when they adopt this lifestyle, which provides a sense of independence and flexibility. Nevertheless, it presents difficulties in terms of internet access, the search for appropriate areas for temporary living, and the requirement to adapt to various surroundings.

There is a growing movement toward living off the grid, known as the tiny house movement. This movement encourages people to live in homes that are small, minimalist, and frequently built on wheels. These residences are designed to maximize space efficiency while limiting their impact on the environment. People living in tiny houses place a high value on simplicity and sustainability, frequently incorporating composting toilets and renewable energy sources into their limited living spaces. The ability to relocate quickly, the reduction in the amount of material consumption, and the lower living costs all contribute to the appeal of this lifestyle. On the other hand, there are difficulties associated with adjusting to living spaces that are considerably smaller and overcoming zoning rules that may restrict the placement of tiny houses.

The seagoing off-grid lifestyle is a lifestyle that symbolizes a concept that combines independence and exploration. People who live on the water, such as sailors and liveaboards, enjoy the experience of sailing or navigating rivers and oceans on sailboats or houseboats. The power they generate comes from the sun or the wind; they collect rainwater to meet their daily requirements and create floating gardens to provide nutrition. A constant change of scenery, a connection to the ocean, and the ability to become self-sufficient via the acquisition of maritime skills are the three factors that contribute to the attractiveness of this way of life. However, there are several obstacles to overcome, including the requirement for maritime expertise, the maintenance of the vessel, and the adjustment to a restricted lifestyle in terms of space and resources.

In conclusion, the wide variety of off-grid lives indicates a widespread yearning for independence, sustainability, and a connection to the natural world. People who embrace off-grid living aim to lower their ecological impact and attain freedom from conventional systems. This dedication is shared regardless of whether they choose the tranquility of a remote cabin, the collaborative spirit of an intentional community, or the mobility of a tiny house on wheels. Whether it be the harsh conditions of living in the wilderness, the hard work of homesteading, the communal dynamics of intentional communities, the adaptability of modern nomads, the compact living of tiny house dwellers, or the maritime skills required for seagoing life, each particular way of life comes with its own distinct set of challenges. These various ways of life collectively contribute to a larger discourse about sustainability, self-sufficiency, and human relationship with the environment. This conversation is fueled by the growing popularity of off-grid living, individually and collectively.

Common Misconceptions

In our complex world, misinformation often thrives, leading to the formation and perpetuation of common misconceptions. These misunderstandings, which may have been formed by gossip, insufficient knowledge, or cultural prejudices, have the potential to impact our perspectives and the decisions that we make. In the interest of promoting a more educated and nuanced understanding, the purpose of this section is to deconstruct and address some common misconceptions pervasive across various domains.

The idea of mental health is the subject of a widespread misunderstanding involving mental health. A persistent stigma is still associated with mental health concerns despite the fact that there has been an increase in understanding and activism for these issues. Many individuals have the mistaken belief that having problems with one's mental health is an indication of personal weakness or a lack of personal perseverance. A person's mental health is the result of a complicated interaction between biological, psychological, and environmental elements. However, it is not a perceived lack of character that is required to acknowledge and seek assistance for mental health difficulties; instead, it is strength and self-awareness that are needed. The elimination of this misunderstanding is essential to provide a setting that is more sympathetic and helpful for people who are struggling with challenges related to their mental health.

There is also a widespread misunderstanding regarding the connection between immunizations and autism. Even though several scientific studies have disproved the existence of a causal connection between vaccinations and autism, there are still some people who continue to hold this idea. The root of this misunderstanding may be traced back to a study that has since been discredited. Yet, its influence has been significant, contributing to vaccine hesitancy and putting public health at risk. Vaccines are a safe and effective method of disease prevention, protecting not only individuals but also vulnerable communities through herd immunity. It is crucial to underline the overwhelming scientific consensus that vaccines are a safe and efficient method of disease prevention.

The assumption that a single frigid winter or a localized weather event may deny the reality of global warming is a prevalent mistake in climate change. This misconception is based on the idea that global warming is occurring. It is necessary to have a comprehensive grasp of climate change since it is caused by consistent long-term trends in temperature, rising sea levels, and catastrophic weather occurrences. Attempting to disprove the vast body of scientific evidence that climate change is occurring by pointing to individual events is analogous to missing the forest rather than the trees. To promote a common understanding of the urgent need for global action to reduce the risks of climate change, it is essential to dispel this myth.

It is very uncommon for the field of psychology to be plagued with misunderstandings, and one of the most widespread myths is the idea that people only employ ten percent of their brains. The field of neuroscience does not provide evidence for this concept, which is widely held in popular culture. Imaging studies of the brain regularly demonstrate that different brain regions are engaged, even when doing tasks that appear to be relatively straightforward. To comprehend the whole range of human cognition and eliminate the myth of untapped mental capacity, it is vital to have a thorough understanding of the complexities and nuances of brain function.

One of the most pervasive fallacies in economics is the notion that the wealth of a nation is primarily defined by its gross domestic product (GDP). This one is among the many misconceptions that exist in economics. The Gross Domestic Product (GDP) is an important economic statistic. Yet, it needs to provide a complete picture of the well-being of a nation or the distribution of financial resources. It is important to note that various factors, including income disparity, social welfare, and environmental sustainability, heavily influence a country's prosperity. Getting to the bottom of the limitations of GDP as a single statistic is essential for policymakers and the general public to make educated judgments regarding the objectives of the economy.

Since the beginning of time, the notion that fat is intrinsically harmful to one's health has been widely believed in nutrition. Even though consuming excessive saturated and trans fats can be detrimental, it is essential to acknowledge the significance of healthy fats in developing a well-balanced diet. Both monounsaturated and polyunsaturated fats, which may be found in foods such as avocados, almonds, and olive oil, are necessary for various biological activities, including maintaining healthy brain function. It is essential to dispel the notion that fat should be banned entirely since it adds to a more sophisticated understanding of nutrition and allows individuals to make informed judgments about their diet.

Within the criminal justice field, one of the most widespread misunderstandings is the notion that the testimony of eyewitnesses is always reliable. Many studies have shed light on the fact that human memory is susceptible to errors, which various factors, including stress, suggestion, and the simple passage of time, can cause. Legal experts, law enforcement, and the general public need to acknowledge the limitations of eyewitness evidence to ensure that the outcomes of judicial proceedings are fair and truthful.

Throughout space research, there has been a persistent belief that black holes act as cosmic vacuum cleaners, consuming everything in their immediate area. Even though black holes are potent gravitational entities, their impact does not extend to every conceivable direction. It is possible for objects in orbit around a black hole, such as stars and gas clouds, to demonstrate steady motion without being absorbed by the black hole right away. To promote a more accurate understanding of these mysterious cosmic occurrences, it is vital to disentangle the popular portrayal of black holes from the truth found in the scientific community.

One of the most widespread misunderstandings in history is the notion that Christopher Columbus began his expedition in 1492 to demonstrate that the Earth appeared to be round. By the time of Christopher Columbus, the concept of a spherical Earth had already gained widespread acceptance among educated Europeans. To disprove the widely held belief that the ocean was treacherous and inaccessible, his endeavor sought to discover a path that led westward to Asia. Correcting this misunderstanding enables one to acquire a more nuanced comprehension of the historical settings and the reasons that led to significant moments in the exploratory process.

A recurring technological fallacy focuses on the assertion that private browsing modes, frequently referred to as "incognito" or "private," offer complete anonymity and privacy. Even though these modes limit the preservation of browsing history on the local device, they do not render users invisible to internet service providers, websites, or possible dangers. For users to be able to make educated judgments regarding the privacy and security measures utilized on the internet, this fallacy must be dispelled.

In conclusion, widespread misunderstandings continue to exist across a variety of domains, which in turn shape our views and influence the decisions that we make. Dispelling these misconceptions demands a dedication to critical thinking, scientific literacy, and a willingness to challenge ingrained views. This is true regardless of whether the topic is mental health, climate change, psychology, economics, nutrition, criminal justice, space exploration, history, or technology. Individuals are given the ability to make informed choices, contribute to meaningful discourse, and navigate an increasingly complicated world with clarity and discernment when they are provided the opportunity to cultivate a more accurate understanding of complex subjects.

CHAPTER II

The Science Behind Off-Grid Systems

Sustainable Energy Sources

In the face of escalating environmental challenges and the relentless depletion of finite fossil fuel reserves, the global pursuit of sustainable energy sources has emerged as a pivotal strategy to ensure our planet's and its inhabitants' well-being. There is an urgent need to reduce dependency on non-renewable resources, mitigate climate change, and build a resilient energy infrastructure, all of which drive the pursuit of sustainable energy. This section investigates the relevance of sustainable energy sources, and a wide range of technologies and practices that potentially transform the future of energy production and use are discussed.

Solar power has emerged as one of the most significant contributors to sustainable energy development. Through the use of photovoltaic cells, the process of capturing energy from the sun's rays has become increasingly efficient and cost-effective. There is a clean and renewable energy source that can be provided by solar panels, regardless of whether they are installed in buildings or enormous solar farms. Solar energy applies to a wide range of settings and geographic areas due to its scalability, which allows it to be installed anywhere from individual rooftops to large-scale solar parks without much difficulty. Solar technology is progressing, so the possibility of mass adoption and integration into preexisting energy infrastructures is becoming increasingly attractive.

In environmentally responsible electricity generation, wind energy is another pillar that stands out. The kinetic energy of the moving air is converted into power by wind turbines, which are deliberately placed in places that experience high wind speeds. During this period, this technology has undergone significant expansion, resulting in the development of towering wind farms both onshore and offshore. Innovative designs and grid integration tactics have been implemented to overcome the visual effect and intermittency difficulties connected with wind power. The outcome of this is that wind energy has developed into a dependable and scalable solution, and it is now capable of meeting a considerable portion of the demand for electricity around the world.

Since the beginning of time, people have been able to utilize hydropower, which is a well-established renewable energy source. Hydroelectric power plants create electricity by operating turbines that are connected to generators. These plants make use of the kinetic energy that is contained within moving water. Even though large-scale dams have caused environmental problems due to the destruction of habitats and the alteration of river ecosystems, run-of-river systems and small-scale hydropower projects provide more environmentally friendly options. In addition, developments in turbine technology and environmental impact studies are leading the creation of hydropower projects that balance the satisfaction of energy requirements and the preservation of ecological systems.

Utilizing the heat inside the Earth, geothermal energy can either be converted into electricity or directly supplied to systems used for heating and cooling. As a result of its regular and reliable output, geothermal power plants are frequently situated in areas characterized by high levels of volcanic activity or geothermal reservoirs. Geothermal power, in contrast to solar and wind energy, is not affected by changes in the weather, making it a reliable source of electricity. The geographic scope of viable geothermal projects is expanding due to advancements in geothermal exploration and drilling technologies. This makes geothermal energy a resource that is becoming increasingly accessible and sustainable for various energy requirements.

The organic matter derived from plants and animals, such as agricultural residues, forestry byproducts, and organic waste, can be utilized to generate energy through biomass conservation. Heat, electricity, or biofuel production can be accomplished by using biomass through processes such as combustion, gasification, or anaerobic digestion. Although biomass has the potential to contribute to carbon neutrality through the recycling of organic carbon, it is essential to manage it with caution to minimize negative repercussions on the environment, such as the destruction of forests and competition with food crops. By combining environmentally responsible practices with technical advancements, biomass has the potential to play a more significant part in the transition to a more environmentally friendly and resilient energy landscape.

Tidal and wave energy are examples of the potential our oceans have yet to realize fully. During the rising and falling tides, tidal power can generate energy by utilizing the gravitational forces between the Earth, the moon, and the sun. Alternatively, wave energy is a form of energy derived from ocean waves' kinetic energy. Compared to conventional hydropower, both types of marine energy provide a reliable and consistent source of power generation while having a minor impact on the surrounding ecosystem. Continuing research and pilot projects point to a potential future for exploiting the massive energy sources contained beneath our oceans. This is even though there are technical obstacles and restricted implementation.

Incorporating renewable energy sources into our global energy mix necessitates the development of innovative technologies, the establishment of comprehensive legislative frameworks, and the raising of public awareness. Governments worldwide play a crucial role in creating an atmosphere favorable for the development and implementation of sustainable energy solutions. It is possible to encourage investment in renewable technology and make the transition from fossil fuels easier by implementing legislative frameworks, financial incentives, and subsidies. Concurrently, public awareness initiatives can potentially educate consumers about the advantages of sustainable energy, fostering widespread adoption and generating market demand for cleaner alternatives.

Over the last ten years, there has been a substantial improvement in the economic feasibility of sustainable energy sources, which has resulted in these sources becoming increasingly competitive with traditional fossil fuels. The business case for renewable energy has been strengthened due to the decreasing costs of some technologies, such as solar panels, wind turbines, and energy storage technologies. Consequently, investments in projects that utilize sustainable energy have increased significantly, garnering the interest of big energy giants and fledgling startups. This trend not only hastens the implementation of environmentally friendly technology but also provides employment opportunities and contributes to the economy's expansion in renewable energy.

In conclusion, the shift to sustainable energy sources is necessary to solve the interconnected problems of climate change, the depletion of resources, and the destruction of the environment. Collectively, the wide variety of renewable technologies, including geothermal and marine energy in addition to solar and wind power, provide a road map toward a more environmentally friendly and sustainable future. However, to make this vision a reality, it will take a coordinated effort on the part of governments, businesses, and individuals to embrace and invest in clean energy solutions. By acting in this manner, we not only ensure the existence of a dependable and robust energy infrastructure, but we also contribute to the well-being of both the current generation and the generations to come on a globe where sustainability is the primary focus.

Water Harvesting and Management

Water, the elixir of life, is a finite resource crucial for the survival of ecosystems, agriculture, industries, and human communities. In light of the increasing pressures brought on by population increase, climate change, and urbanization, it has become necessary to implement efficient water harvesting and management practices to guarantee this valuable resource's equitable distribution, conservation, and long-term viability. This section dives into the myriad of facets comprising water harvesting and management, examining the various approaches and technologies that contribute to preserving water availability for both the current generation and those to come in the future.

When taken in its broadest sense, water harvesting

refers to collecting and storing rainwater, surface runoff, and groundwater to satisfy various requirements. Rainwater harvesting, in particular, has become increasingly popular as a sustainable activity using abundant precipitation in many places. Communities can lessen their reliance on traditional water sources by gathering rainwater through catchment systems such as gutters, rooftops, and other systems. Rainwater harvesting helps prevent urban flooding and soil erosion caused by excessive runoff and provides a decentralized and locally available water supply. Rainwater harvesting makes all of these benefits available.

In the agricultural industry, which is highly dependent

on water, new water collecting systems are essential in promoting a sustainable farming practice. Methods such as conservation tillage, agroforestry, and contour plowing are examples of practices that improve water retention in soil, hence lowering the amount of water that runs off and increasing the amount of groundwater recharged. In addition, implementing precision irrigation technologies, such as drip and sprinkler systems, enables farmers to maximize crop productivity while avoiding water waste and optimizing water usage. There is a correlation between incorporating these practices into agricultural landscapes and water conservation and an improvement in the resistance to climatic unpredictability.

For various reasons, including agricultural, industrial, and domestic uses, groundwater is frequently extracted. Groundwater is an essential component of the worldwide water cycle. Nevertheless, extraction methods that could be more sustainable have resulted in the depletion of aquifers in several different regions. MAR, which stands for managed aquifer recharge, is increasingly recognized as a strategic method for replenishing subsurface water reservoirs. Intentional recharging of aquifers is accomplished through the injection of surface water or wastewater treated in the process of MAR. In addition to restoring groundwater levels, this also improves water quality by facilitating natural filtration processes, improving water quality. It is possible to maintain a sustainable equilibrium between the extraction of groundwater and recharge through prudent management of groundwater resources using methods such as aquifer storage and recovery (ASR).

While urbanization is a significant driver of economic growth, it also presents considerable problems in managing water resources. Rapid urban expansion frequently results in the formation of impervious surfaces, which act as a barrier to the natural penetration of water and increase the amount of runoff from the surface. Rainwater harvesting, stormwater management, and wastewater treatment are all components of integrated urban water management, which provides a comprehensive solution. Porous pavements and green roofs are examples of green infrastructure that may absorb rainwater and reduce runoff, reducing the risk of urban flooding and increasing groundwater recharging. As an additional benefit, decentralized wastewater treatment systems recycle and reuse water, reducing the strain on conventional water supply sources.

The ancient methods of water collecting have been used to support people for millennia in arid and semi-arid regions characterized by a severe lack of available water. Old methods such as constructing check dams, contour trenches, and rooftop water collection systems are examples of the wisdom of efficiently using water resources to make the most of limited water resources. There are practical alternatives available for water-scarce areas, and these solutions include modern adaptations of these historic approaches and technological advances. A solid framework for the sustainable gathering and management of water in demanding contexts is formed by the resuscitation of traditional knowledge, which, combined with contemporary innovations, contributes to the formation of this framework.

The precipitation patterns, water flow regulation, and water quality maintenance are all subject to the influence of ecosystems, which play a crucial part in the water cycle. A holistic approach to managing complete drainage basins, an ecosystem-based approach, is the primary focus of watershed management. Preservation and restoration of natural vegetation in watersheds contribute to the prevention of soil erosion, the enhancement of water infiltration, and the maintenance of biodiversity. Conservation of wetland areas, which are essential components of many watersheds, contributes to preventing flooding, replenishing groundwater, and purifying water. The necessity of adopting policies prioritizing ecological integrity is highlighted by the fact that it is essential to acknowledge the inherent connection between healthy ecosystems and water availability.

Water shortage is not a problem confined to a particular place; instead, it is a worldwide problem made worse by climate change. Adaptive methods are required worldwide because of the unpredictable nature of precipitation, the increased frequency of droughts, and the changing patterns of hydrological processes. Implementing climate-resilient water collection and management strategies is necessary to construct adaptive capacity and guarantee water security in the face of a changing climate. This includes the creation of early warning systems, climate-smart infrastructure, and policies that incorporate climate considerations into the water resource management design.

Water harvesting and management constitute a dynamic and interdisciplinary area that handles the numerous water scarcity, degradation, and climate change difficulties. To construct robust water systems that meet the varied requirements of ecosystems and communities, it is vital to incorporate both traditional knowledge and modern advancements, as well as sustainable practices. The diversity of accessible techniques exemplifies the versatility and adaptation required to navigate the changing water landscape. These strategies range from collecting rainwater in urban areas to using precision irrigation in agriculture and ecosystem-based watershed management. Humanity can usher in a new era in which water is revered, preserved, and shared sustainably for the benefit of all people if everyone adopts a comprehensive and collaborative approach.

Waste Management

Waste management is a critical challenge in the modern era, marked by escalating population growth, urbanization, and consumption patterns that generate vast amounts of discarded materials. In addition to being essential for preserving the environment, the efficient management of trash is also critical to maintaining public health and the long-term viability of ecosystems. In this section, the multiple aspects of waste management are investigated. The study delves into the intricacies of waste generation, disposal, and recycling and the growing techniques that attempt to create a circular economy that minimizes the environmental impact.

The magnitude of garbage created on a worldwide scale is astonishing. The amount of municipal solid garbage, industrial waste, and electronic waste has increased significantly as a result of the increasing prevalence of consumer-driven lifestyles in countries. In the past, landfills were the dominant answer for garbage disposal; however, they are presently under excessive stress and contribute to the destruction of the ecosystem. The 'take, make, dispose' approach is unsustainable, which has led to a paradigm shift towards a circular economy. This model emphasizes resource efficiency, recycling, and reducing waste generation from the very beginning of the process.

One of the most important aspects of waste management systems is handling municipal solid waste (MSW). It comprises various items, such as garbage from commercial and institutional establishments, waste from businesses, and waste from households. Trash reduction at the source through knowledge and behavioral change, reuse of products, recycling of materials, and appropriate disposal of residual trash are the methods that make up an effective management system for municipal solid waste (MSW). Other techniques include recycling of materials. Incineration and anaerobic digestion are two examples of waste-to-energy technologies that provide alternatives for extracting energy from garbage while limiting the environmental impact. However, these technologies come with their own unique set of obstacles and debates.

One of the most critical aspects of environmentally responsible trash management is recycling. The goal of the recycling business is to convert materials that have been wasted into raw materials that can be used in the production of new products. This helps to reduce the demand for virgin resources and slow down the destruction of the environment. Paper, glass, metals, and plastics are several examples of items that are frequently recycled. However, difficulties continue to exist, particularly in the recycling of plastics, which is a problem due to the wide variety of polymer types and the contamination of recyclable waste streams. When it comes to maximizing the recycling cycle, it is vital to have innovations in recycling technologies and public awareness programs that promote responsible garbage disposal.

Electronic garbage, also known as e-waste, presents a one-of-a-kind obstacle in the context of the modern waste management landscape. The rapid speed of technological advancement causes electronic equipment to become obsolete quickly, which in turn results in an increasing amount of electronic waste available for disposal. Because electronic trash contains potentially harmful substances, such as heavy metals and toxic compounds, incorrect disposal of this waste is a significant cause for worry in terms of both public health and the environment. The recovery of valuable materials and reducing the negative influence of electronic devices on the environment are responsible for e-waste management's goals, including recycling and correct disposal.

In its most fundamental form, waste management calls for a transition from a linear economy to a circular economy. The circular economy model emphasizes decreasing waste generation by implementing environmentally responsible industrial processes. It also encourages the design of products that make recycling and reuse easier. Extended producer responsibility (EPR) procedures ensure that manufacturers are held accountable for their goods' life cycles, beginning with their design and ending with their disposal. Internalizing the environmental costs associated with their products incentivizes manufacturers to adopt environmentally friendly methods, which in turn fosters a more sustainable approach to consumption and waste management.

The term "waste management" encompasses the more conventional focus on municipal garbage and the more general concept of resource management. 'Waste' is undergoing a process of redefining itself as cultures investigate methods to derive value from items that were previously considered to be disposable. The idea of a circular economy challenges the concept of waste. It envisions a system in which materials are continuously cycled and reused, leaving a tiny place for garbage to be considered waste. Consumers, industry, and governments must work together to rethink production and consumption habits for this paradigm shift. This will result in creating a regenerative system that reduces the negative impact on the environment.

More and more people are realizing that landfills, traditionally the principal location for garbage disposal, are not sustainable and are harmful to the environment. Land is becoming increasingly scarce, and the environmental impacts of landfills are becoming more apparent. As a result, alternative means of trash disposal are becoming increasingly popular. Incineration is one example of a waste-to-energy technology that aims to generate electricity from waste materials while lowering the amount of waste disposed of in landfills. Concerns regarding air pollution, emissions of greenhouse gases, and the possibility of the discharge of toxic byproducts highlight the necessity of tight laws and constant technological improvements to reduce these methods' negative impact on the environment.

Waste management is a technical difficulty and a social and cultural challenge. One of the most critical factors in garbage production and disposal is consumer behavior, heavily influenced by advertising and the need for convenience. Developing a culture of responsible trash disposal and educating the general people about the environmental effects of their consumption decisions are essential components of sustainable waste management methods. Contributing to the formation of a more environmentally conscious society are initiatives that encourage recycling habits, prohibit the use of things that are only intended for a single use, and promote waste reduction at the source.

Collaborative and integrated approaches are required to meet the issues associated with waste management on a global scale. The Basel Convention on the Control of Transboundary Movements of Hazardous Wastes and Their Disposal is one example of an international agreement that serves as a framework for controlling the movement of hazardous waste across international borders and fostering global collaboration. The collective capacity to address the challenges of waste management on a worldwide scale can be increased by sharing best practices, technologies, and knowledge across international borders.

In conclusion, waste management is a complex problem that calls for an all-encompassing and integrated method. To reduce the adverse effects that waste has on the environment, it is necessary to make the shift from a linear economy to a circular economy, as well as to make progress in recycling technologies and implement appropriate trash disposal methods. It has never been more important for communities to embrace sustainable consumption patterns, limit the waste they generate, and encourage circular economies than now, as civilizations struggle to deal with the repercussions of a culture that values disability. We can pave the road for a more sustainable and resilient future if we redefine our relationship with garbage and embrace creative solutions.

Sustainable Building Practices

In the face of escalating environmental concerns and the ever-growing impact of climate change, sustainable building practices have emerged as a beacon of hope, offering a pathway toward a more ecologically conscious and resilient future. These practices comprise a wide range of approaches, materials, and designs made to reduce the environmental imprint of buildings and promote ecological harmony over the long term. Sustainable building practices are not only a trend; they represent a significant paradigm shift in architecture and construction. These practices pose a challenge to the conventional standards that have been established and encourage a reassessment of our connection with the built environment.

The notion of green building, which is an approach that stresses resource efficiency, energy conservation, and the use of environmentally friendly materials, is at the core of the philosophy that underpins sustainable building practices. Green buildings are constructed to minimize the negative consequences of construction on ecosystems, maximizing the efficiency with which energy is consumed and minimizing waste. Using cutting-edge technology and designs to reduce energy consumption and, as a result, carbon emissions is an essential component of sustainable construction. Energy efficiency is a cornerstone of sustainable building. The adoption of energy-efficient appliances and insulation materials, as well as the incorporation of renewable energy sources like solar panels and wind turbines, are all items that fall under this category.

Regarding environmentally responsible building techniques, the selection of materials is of the utmost significance. Concrete and steel are two examples of traditional building materials that frequently substantially influence the environment due to the extraction of resources, the production processes, and the transportation of these materials. The goal of sustainable building is to find a solution to this problem by encouraging the use of environmentally friendly materials that have a lower embodied energy and are sourced responsibly. In the building industry, bamboo, for example, is a rapidly regenerated material that can be utilized for various uses. It provides a sustainable alternative to traditional hardwoods. In addition, recycled and reclaimed materials, such as recycled steel and recovered wood, are becoming increasingly popular in sustainable building methods. These materials contribute to the reduction of waste and the conservation of resources.

Water conservation is yet another essential component of environmentally responsible building techniques. Since water scarcity is a pressing global concern, green building designs integrate efforts to limit water usage. These tactics include implementing water-efficient fixtures, rainwater harvesting systems, and greywater recycling. Implementing these techniques not only lessens the impact that sustainable buildings have on the water resources in their immediate vicinity, but it also contributes to the broader conservation and responsible management of water.

In sustainable practices, the lifecycle of a building is an essential factor to consider once the construction process has concluded. Evaluating the long-term operational efficiency, the maintenance requirements, and the possibilities for adaptive reuse or recycling of materials are all part of this process. By designing buildings with flexibility and adaptability, it is possible to ensure that they can develop with changing needs, decreasing the need for demolition and new construction if the buildings are designed. In addition, incorporating intelligent technology, such as energy management systems and automated controls, improves the operational efficiency of buildings, further reducing the impact of these structures on the environment.

As sustainable construction methods continue to gain popularity, the notion of biophilic design is gaining ground. This design concept emphasizes incorporating nature and natural materials into the built environment. Blending components such as green roofs, living walls, and enough natural light into building designs is an example of biophilic design, which acknowledges humans' inherent connection with the natural world and aims to improve well-being throughout the building. In addition to improving the quality of life, biophilic design also contributes to preserving the environment by lowering the amount of artificial lighting, heating, and cooling required. This is accomplished by establishing a harmonious relationship between the people who live in the building and the natural surroundings.

Engagement with the community and a sense of social responsibility are integral to sustainable building practices. The aim of sustainable buildings is not only to provide environmental benefits but also to foster a sense of belonging by creating healthy and welcoming communities. This involves considering various factors during the design and construction process, including accessibility, cost, and the community's cultural context. Moreover, sustainable building approaches often emphasize using local labor and materials, contributing to the economic growth of the community adjacent to the project.

A significant contribution to the promotion and acceleration of adopting sustainable construction methods is made by the policies and incentives implemented by the government. Several nations and municipalities encourage the construction and development industries to emphasize sustainability by providing tax incentives, subsidies, and certification schemes. For instance, the Leadership in Energy and Environmental Design (LEED) certification has developed into a standard generally acknowledged for assessing the environmental performance of buildings. These certifications serve as a baseline for sustainable practices and as a marketing tool, as increasing numbers of people concerned about the environment are looking for ecologically friendly and energy-efficient buildings.

Although there has been a steady increase in the use of sustainable building principles, there are still hurdles that need to be overcome to mainstream these approaches. Because early investments in environmentally friendly technology and materials can be more than those in conventional alternatives, cost considerations frequently present a barrier. Nevertheless, it is of utmost importance to acknowledge that the long-term benefits, including decreased operational expenses, increased property value, and positive environmental impacts, surpass the initial financial restraints. The cost differentials are expected to decrease as technology continues to evolve, and economies of scale come into play. This will make sustainable building methods more affordable to a broader variety of homeowners and developers.

In conclusion, sustainable building practices represent a holistic construction approach that transcends traditional design and development paradigms. By focusing on resource efficiency, energy conservation, and environmental stewardship, these practices offer a hopeful path toward reducing the negative impact of construction activities on the environment. Given the urgent global need for sustainable solutions to combat climate change and preserve our planet, adopting and promoting sustainable building methods is not just a choice but a hopeful commitment to a greener, healthier, and more resilient future. Environmentally responsible building techniques have the potential to pave the way for a harmonious coexistence between human habitats and the natural world, achievable through a combination of technological innovation, community involvement, and regulatory support.

CHAPTER III

The Art of Off-Grid Living

Designing Your Off-Grid Home

Living off the grid has gained traction in recent years as individuals seek alternatives to traditional urban and suburban living. The interest in creating off-grid homes has been spurred by the appeal of independence from centralized power sources, decreased environmental impact, and a deeper connection to nature compared to conventional living arrangements. To construct a self-sufficient house in terms of operation, relying on renewable energy sources and environmentally responsible practices, it is necessary to engage in careful planning and implement innovative design. The process of designing an off-grid home involves more than simply the generation of electricity; it is a comprehensive strategy that takes into account the production of energy, the management of water, the disposal of trash, and the general resilience of the structure to guarantee a self-sufficient and sustainable way of living.

Selecting a suitable location is one of the fundamental aspects that must be considered while developing an off-grid house. Essential considerations include choosing a location that receives a sufficient amount of sunshine for solar power, having access to water sources, and considering the area's climate conditions. It is common practice to choose a south-facing orientation since it allows for the most efficient positioning of solar panels and passive solar heating systems, thereby receiving the maximum amount of sunshine possible. A significant component of off-grid living is the simplification of water collection and administration, which can be accomplished by proximity to bodies of water or the availability of subsurface water sources. In addition, awareness of the local climate is beneficial when constructing a house that resists severe weather conditions while providing a comfortable living environment.

Living off the grid is based on the principle of energy independence, and using renewable energy sources is essential in accomplishing this objective. Photovoltaic panels that collect energy from the sun are a form of solar power that is becoming increasingly common. To derive the most significant possible amount of sunshine throughout the day, the design must consider the positioning and direction of these panels. In regions that see constant wind patterns, wind turbines can serve as a complementary source of clean energy to solar power, offering an extra energy source. The kinetic energy of water can be converted into electricity through micro-hydro devices, which can be installed in areas where water is flowing. Incorporating several different renewable energy sources into a single system, commonly known as a hybrid system, improves dependability and guarantees a consistent electricity supply, regardless of weather conditions.

The intermittent nature of renewable energy sources necessitates utilizing energy storage as an essential component of off-grid life. Batteries, such as lithium-ion or lead-acid batteries, can effectively store surplus energy generated during moments of peak production. This energy can be utilized later when energy generation is either low or nonexistent. The battery's capacity, the rate at which it charges and discharges, and the overall energy demand of the family are all factors that must be considered when designing an efficient energy storage system. In addition, the incorporation of energy-efficient appliances and lighting systems results in a reduction in overall energy consumption, which in turn makes the off-grid system more environmentally friendly and cost-effective.

Water management is another essential component in the construction of off-grid homes. It is only sometimes guaranteed that those living off the grid will have access to a water source that is both dependable and safe. A sustainable alternative is provided by rainwater harvesting, which involves collecting and storing rainwater for usage in residential settings. To ensure that the water is high quality, the design should incorporate sufficient roof space to collect rainwater and storage tanks fitted with filtration devices. Greywater recycling systems have the potential to further improve the water economy by cleaning and reusing water from household appliances such as washing machines, sinks, and showers for non-potable purposes such as irrigation applications. This project aims to establish a closed-loop water system that minimizes dependency on external water sources and lessens the environmental impact of water usage.

In an off-grid environment, waste management requires reducing trash as much as possible and adopting disposal practices that benefit the environment. In the case of composting toilets, for instance, human waste is transformed into compost rich in nutrients, removing the requirement for conventional sewage systems. Recycling and reusing materials are essential components of off-grid life since they significantly reduce the need for new resources and minimize the negative impact of trash on the environment. A lower ecological footprint can be achieved by designing the home with an emphasis on sustainable materials, such as reclaimed wood, recycled metal, and low-impact insulation. This aligns with the ideals of off-grid living and ensures a smaller overall footprint.

Architectural design is significant in creating a comfortable and energy-efficient off-grid home. Passive solar design is an essential factor to take into consideration. This design strategy involves optimizing the positioning of windows, thermal mass, and insulation to catch and retain solar heat. Active heating or cooling systems are less required when this design style is utilized because it helps manage the temperatures within. Adequate insulation is necessary to keep the temperature within the building at a reasonable level and maximize energy efficiency. In addition, the utilization of natural ventilation, accomplished by strategically positioning windows and ventilation systems, guarantees a continuous flow of fresh air without the need for energy-intensive air conditioning.

The incorporation of smart home technology has the potential to improve the level of efficiency and ease of living off the grid. Homeowners can monitor and control their energy consumption, temperature, and security systems from any location thanks to energy management systems, home automation, and remote monitoring. Utilizing resources in the most efficient manner possible and offering real-time insights into the operation of renewable energy systems are two ways these technologies contribute to energy conservation. Furthermore, smart home technologies can improve the overall resilience of off-grid homes by delivering early warnings and making it easier to perform remote troubleshooting if the system begins to malfunction.

The concepts of off-grid living are perfectly aligned with the notion of permaculture, which is a way of life that incorporates sustainable agriculture, land usage, and community design. The building of a home that is in harmony with the surrounding landscape, the incorporation of edible landscaping, and the cultivation of a garden that can sustain itself all contribute to the reduction of the need for external resources and the enhancement of food security. The principles of permaculture also emphasize the significance of biodiversity, which helps foster an ecosystem that is resilient and able to resist changes and disruptions in the surrounding environment.

Participation in the community and the exchange of information are essential parts of off-grid living. People can communicate with one another, share resources, and work together to find solutions to problems when they become members of off-grid communities or build their own. Participating in workshops, gaining knowledge from the experiences of others, and keeping up with the latest developments in off-grid technology are all factors that contribute to the continued success and sustainability of off-grid life.

In conclusion, building a home that is off-grid is a

multifaceted activity involving more than just disconnecting from public utilities. Taking into consideration energy, water, trash, and architectural design in a way that is both deliberate and integrated is required. For off-grid living to be successful, it is essential to consider the local environment, renewable energy sources, water management measures, and sustainable building practices. Individuals cancan construct homes that not only fulfill their immediate needs but also contribute to a more sustainable and regenerative future if they incorporate the values of independence, resilience, and environmental stewardship into their design strategy. At a time when the world is struggling to cope with the problems of climate change and the depletion of resources, off-grid living demonstrates the possibilities of humans and their environment living together in harmony.

Choosing the Right Location

The significance of location in any aspect of life cannot be overstated, and when it comes to real estate, it becomes a paramount consideration. Location can significantly impact many aspects of one's life and financial well-being, including where to live, establish a business, or invest in property. When selecting the ideal site, the process involves a complicated interaction between individual preferences, economic considerations, and potential future outcomes. It requires striking a delicate balance between meeting immediate needs and considering long-term issues. It can influence both the quality of life and the performance of investments.

When it comes to residential real estate, decisions frequently revolve around the search for the perfect place to call home. Many elements influence the selection of a neighborhood, town, or city, the first of which is the individual's preferences about their way of life. Many prioritize being close to their places of employment, schools, and other facilities. The ability to commute to work from a location easily accessible to major highways or public transportation can substantially impact the daily commute and contribute to a better work-life balance. In addition, the quality of the schools in the region is an essential factor, particularly for families who have children, because education is the main factor considered during the decision-making process.

Safety and security must be considered when selecting a residential site. Crime rates, neighborhood watch programs, and a region's strong sense of community all contribute to the overall feeling of safety in that place. It is possible to gain significant insights into a potential location's safety by researching crime data and participating in community projects. Because environmental elements, such as the air and water quality, also contribute to the general well-being of residents, it is vital to consider the environmental conditions of a location being considered.

Some of the most critical factors that contribute to the allure of a location are its cultural and recreational offerings. Individuals looking for a more enriching lifestyle frequently visit vibrant areas with cultural attractions, parks, and recreational facilities. The availability of green areas, entertainment venues, and community events can improve overall quality of life. Additionally, the availability of healthcare facilities, retail complexes, and food alternatives are all factors that add to the convenience and popularity of a location.

One of the most important factors to consider when selecting a residential location is the economy, particularly regarding the cost of living and the property's value. It is directly influenced by factors such as the cost of living, property taxes, and home prices, whether or not it is financially feasible to reside in a specific place. When a region's economic stability and growth prospects are evaluated, it is possible to gain insights into the prospective appreciation of property values over time. In addition, a grasp of the local employment market and economic diversity can impact long-term decisions, particularly for individuals contemplating the purchase of a home as an investment.

Launching a new enterprise entails many factors when choosing the appropriate site for a business. The demand in the market, the level of competition, and the regulatory environment are all elements that become extremely important for entrepreneurs. A considerable impact on a business's operational efficiency and logistics can be brought about by its closeness to suppliers, distributors, and target customers. In addition, zoning rules and local business policies are considered when deciding whether or not it is feasible to start and operate a firm in a particular location.

Demographic factors are critical when locating a domestic business or a commercial enterprise. Individuals can be assisted in making decisions based on their tastes and values by understanding a particular region's population density, age demographics, and cultural mix. Businesses need to do a comprehensive analysis of the target market as well as the behavior of consumers. It is necessary to analyze the purchasing power, lifestyle preferences, and requirements of the local people to customize products and services to meet those requirements.

The location of a property is inextricably linked to the decisions made regarding real estate investments. Properties that have the potential to increase in value and offer a favorable return on investment are what investors look for in geographic regions. The panorama of investment opportunities is impacted by a region's economic indicators, including the rate of job growth, demographic trends, and the number of new infrastructure projects. To identify prospects for capital appreciation and rental income, investors can analyze a real estate market's supply and demand dynamics. In addition, the overall economic stability and regulatory environment of a location influence an investment's risk profile.

The climate is an essential factor that must be considered when selecting the ideal site. The weather conditions of a region directly impact the way of life and health of the people who live there. There are some people who enjoy the warmth of tropical climates, while there are others who are drawn to the shifting seasons that temperate regions give them. Because temperature extremes determine the requirements for heating and cooling, the local climate also affects the amount of energy consumed by the environment. In particular, those interested in settling in certain geographical regions should consider the dangers associated with natural disasters, such as hurricanes, earthquakes, or floods. These are extra concerns that should be carefully considered.

The potential for future growth and development inside the organization heavily influences the decision-making process. It is common for individuals and investors searching for long-term prospects to be drawn to locations with planned infrastructure projects, enhanced transportation networks, and a track record of sustained development. Municipal planning and zoning regulations can provide insights into the vision and commitment of local authorities to support growth and sustainability. These regulations can be found in all municipalities. In addition, individuals are better able to make educated decisions on the future worth and livability of a location when they have a better awareness of the possibility of urbanization or rural growth in the surrounding areas.

When selecting the ideal site, personal tastes and urgent requirements are important considerations; nonetheless, it is essential to have a forward-thinking strategy. A decision about one's location can have long-term repercussions that can affect not only one's quality of life but also their financial well-being. Conducting in-depth study, seeking the guidance of professionals, and taking into account both current and future circumstances are all essential components in making educated judgments that align with one's personal objectives and objectives.

In conclusion, selecting the appropriate site is a complex procedure that involves carefully considering various elements. A person's location becomes the backdrop against which their day-to-day existence develops, regardless of whether they choose a place to live, begin a business, or make real estate investments. Several factors contribute to a particular location's overall experience and outcomes. These factors include choices for lifestyle, economic considerations, and plans for the future. When navigating the complexity of location decisions, taking a balanced and informed approach is essential. This strategy ensures that the chosen location aligns with personal objectives and lays the groundwork for a fulfilling and lucrative future.

Incorporating Nature into Your Living Space

As urbanization continues to shape the modern landscape, the longing for a connection to nature has become more pronounced. Consequently, in response to this need, an increasing number of people are looking for ways to bring the outside inside, blurring the borders between internal and exterior environments. Incorporating elements of nature into your living space is not only a design trend; it is a deliberate effort to promote well-being, improve aesthetics, and establish a healthy balance between the natural world and the built environment. This attempt comprises intelligent design, innovative use of materials, and a holistic approach to interior environments that goes beyond aesthetics to impact mental and physical health positively.

Applying biophilic design concepts is one of the most fundamental ways to incorporate elements of nature into the living area. Biophilia, a word coined by biologist Edward O. Wilson, refers to the intrinsic human attraction to nature. Utilizing this relationship, biophilic design incorporates natural aspects, patterns, and materials into the built world to create a more harmonious atmosphere. Large windows that frame external views, living green walls, and indoor plants are common aspects of biophilic architecture. The presence of natural light, essential to the concept of biophilia, not only lights places but also has a beneficial effect on mood and circadian rhythms. Creating an atmosphere conducive to well-being can be accomplished by designing living spaces with an awareness of the natural components that inspire a sense of peace and connection to others.

One of the most important ways to bring nature into the home is through indoor plants. The natural air purification properties of plants and their visual appeal contribute to improving the quality of the air we breathe. Several common houseplants, including peace lilies, spider plants, and snake plants, are well-known for their capacity to remove contaminants from the air and improve the air quality inside the home. Creating a natural environment that is both diverse and visually engaging can be accomplished by incorporating several different plant species into various rooms. Additionally, the process of caring for plants may be a therapeutic and fulfilling experience, which adds a layer of well-being to the living area by adding this layer.

A seamless link to nature can be created within the limits of interior spaces by utilizing natural materials, which play a crucial part in this process. Timber, stone, and natural fibers can evoke feelings of genuineness and coziness. The utilization of reclaimed or repurposed wood not only lends an air of rustic allure to the design but also conforms to sustainable design principles. Exposed brick walls, stone counters, and wooden flooring create a tactile and visually pleasing setting. A commitment to sustainability and a conscious effort to minimize the ecological footprint of the living space is reflected in the selection of natural materials, which goes beyond the aesthetics of the space.

A further enhancement of the integration of nature can be achieved through the layout and design of various indoor areas. Open floor plans that create a sense of flow and a seamless connection between the different living areas represent the organic interconnectedness in natural environments. Creating a sense of connectedness to one's surroundings can be accomplished by strategically positioning furniture in such a way as to maximize views of outdoor vegetation, water features, or natural light fixtures. Additionally, incorporating elements such as fireplaces or water features into the interior design enables the addition of a sensory dimension, which engages inhabitants with the elements' soothing noises and visual attractiveness.

A key strategy for creating a living space that is bright, airy, and inviting is to make the most of the available natural light. Glass doors, skylights, and large windows all act as conduits that allow natural light to penetrate the interior spaces of a building. In addition to lowering the amount of artificial lighting required, this also contributes to an overall improvement in the area's mood. It has been demonstrated that exposure to daylight benefits mood, boosts productivity, and helps regulate circadian rhythms. Creating a visually engaging and harmonious environment may be accomplished by strategically arranging living rooms to capture sunlight at different times of the day. This will ensure a dynamic interplay between light and shadow, which brings about the desired effect.

Incorporating water elements into interior spaces, whether modest indoor fountains, aquariums, or water sculptures mounted on the wall, provides a calming and fascinating element. The soothing effect of the sound of running water is one factor contributing to the overall quiet ambiance. Water features also function as focal points, which helps to establish a sense of connectedness to the natural world. In addition, the reflected qualities of water can improve the visualization of space, giving the impression that spaces are broader and more open than they are. When thoughtfully included in a biophilic design, water elements become essential beyond the visual to engage numerous senses.

Using natural colors is a subtle yet dramatic method to imbue the living area with a sense of nature. These earthy tones, which include greens, browns, and blues, conjure up the hues present in natural settings, producing a peaceful and grounded ambiance. Adding visual interest and excitement to the area can be accomplished by highlighting these hues with occasional splashes of bold colors inspired by flowers or greenery. It is possible to extend the color palette to include furniture, elements of decor, and even textiles, resulting in an aesthetic consistent and inspired by nature throughout the entire home.

To successfully incorporate natural elements into living spaces, creating seamless transitions between indoor and outdoor areas is essential. When the interior and outside of a building are connected by sliding glass doors, French doors, or folding patio doors that open to outdoor regions, the distinction between the two is blurred. This innovative approach to design improves the perception of space and fosters a sense of connection to the natural environment. Patios, decks, and gardens are outdoor living spaces that can be considered extensions of the inside rooms. These places have the potential to offer possibilities for leisure, entertainment, and connection with nature.

When you include nature in your living space, you take a holistic approach that considers the well-being of the people occupying the place. This goes beyond aesthetics and design concepts. The positive effects of exposure to nature on mental health, stress reduction, and overall cognitive performance have been the subject of significant research. Indoor areas constructed to incorporate elements of nature add to a feeling of equilibrium and peace. Together, the visual connection to greenery, the tactile sensation of natural materials, and the sensory engagement with components like water and light all contribute to creating an atmosphere that is beneficial to both physical and mental health.

In addition to the benefits that individuals experience, the integration of natural elements into living spaces is in line with more significant sustainability objectives. A commitment to choosing environmentally friendly materials, designing with energy efficiency in mind, and maintaining a link to the natural environment are all factors that demonstrate a knowledge of the impact that the built environment has on the environment. Sustainable living becomes a physical reality When translated into the design and functionality of living spaces that merge seamlessly with the natural world. Sustainable living is not only an ethos; it becomes a tangible reality.

Bringing elements of nature into your living environment is an undertaking that is both intentional and transformative, and it goes beyond the trends that are seen in interior design. Creating habitats that promote well-being, encourage a connection to nature, and contribute to a more sustainable way of life is a choice that is made consciously. The objective is to create living spaces that can inspire, rejuvenate, and provide a respite from the demands of modern life. This can be accomplished by applying biophilic design principles, utilizing natural materials, or strategically integrating elements such as plants and water features. Incorporating nature into living spaces becomes a powerful monument to the everlasting human need for harmony with the natural world. This desire is fueled by individuals seeking shelter in the peacefulness of nature within their own homes.

Cultivating a Mindset of Simplicity

In a world inundated with information, distractions, and a relentless pursuit of more, simplicity has emerged as a guiding philosophy for those seeking clarity and purpose. The cultivation of a mindset of simplicity requires individuals to make a conscious effort to detach themselves from the complexities of contemporary life. This encourages individuals to concentrate on what is truly important and discover fulfillment in having fewer things. This mindset extends beyond decluttering physical spaces; it encompasses a holistic approach to life that values intentionality, mindfulness, and an appreciation for the beauty of simplicity in all its forms.

At its core, simplicity is about stripping away the non-essential and embracing the essential. In a consumer-driven society that often equates success with material wealth and possessions, adopting a mindset of simplicity challenges conventional notions of achievement. The minimalist movement, which gained prominence in the 21st century, exemplifies this ethos by advocating for intentional living, focusing on experiences over possessions. Minimalism encourages individuals to declutter their physical and mental lives, freeing up space for meaningful connections, experiences, and personal growth.

One of the fundamental aspects of cultivating a mindset of simplicity is decluttering the physical environment. Our living spaces often accumulate excess stuff, resulting in visual noise and a sense of overwhelm.

Embracing minimalism in the home involves purposefully evaluating each possession, keeping only what adds value or brings joy. Decluttering not only creates a more organized and aesthetically pleasing living space but also serves as a metaphor for letting go of the unnecessary baggage that clutters our minds.

Beyond the tangible aspects of decluttering, a mindset of simplicity extends to the digital realm. In an age where technology permeates every aspect of our lives, digital clutter has become a significant source of stress and distraction. Managing emails, notifications, and constant information can be overwhelming. Embracing simplicity in the digital space involves consciously curating online content, decluttering digital devices, and setting boundaries to prevent constant connectivity from encroaching on moments of solitude and reflection.

While simplicity is often associated with the external aspects of life, it is equally applicable to the internal landscape of thoughts and emotions. Cultivating a mindset of simplicity involves decluttering the mind from the constant noise of worry, anxiety, and unnecessary mental chatter. Practices such as mindfulness meditation, deep breathing exercises, and intentional moments of silence can help quiet the mind and create space for clarity and insight. The simplicity of thought makes it possible to approach life in a more focused and present manner, which in turn helps to cultivate a greater sense of calm and inner peace.

The pursuit of simplicity is intertwined with the concept of intentional living. Intentionality involves aligning one's actions with personal values and consciously choosing how to spend time and resources. In a world where busyness is often equated with productivity, intentional living challenges the notion that more is always better. It encourages individuals to prioritize activities that align with their values and contribute to a sense of purpose and fulfillment. By saying no to the extra, individuals can make room for the meaningful and create a life that reflects their authentic priorities.

Simplicity is not synonymous with austerity; it is about prioritizing quality over quantity. This applies to various aspects of life, from the possessions we choose to the relationships we cultivate. In the consumer-driven culture, there is a growing awareness of the environmental impact of overconsumption. Adopting a mindset of simplicity involves making mindful choices about the products we buy, considering their ecological footprint and long-term sustainability. Quality possessions that stand the test of time often hold more value than disposable items.

Cultivating a simple mindset also extends to how we approach time and commitments. The busyness epidemic has led to a constant juggling of responsibilities, often at the expense of personal well-being. Embracing simplicity in time management involves prioritizing activities that bring joy and fulfillment and contribute to personal growth. This may mean saying no to unnecessary commitments, creating boundaries, and allowing for moments of rest and rejuvenation. Simplicity in time and commitments fosters a healthier work-life balance and reduces the stress associated with an overloaded schedule.

The practice of gratitude is a cornerstone of a mindset of simplicity. Gratitude shifts the focus from what is lacking to what is present, encouraging individuals to appreciate the simple joys and blessings in their lives. Cultivating a habit of expressing gratitude through daily reflections or gratitude journals reinforces a positive mindset and fosters contentment with the present moment. Gratitude is a powerful antidote to the constant pursuit of more, reminding individuals of the richness of their current experiences and relationships.

In relationships, simplicity involves fostering genuine connections and prioritizing quality over quantity. The digital age has facilitated a vast network of virtual connections, but the depth of these relationships is often diluted. Cultivating a mindset of simplicity in relationships means valuing meaningful connections and investing time and energy in those that bring joy, support, and mutual growth. Simplicity in relationships emphasizes the importance of presence, active listening, and shared experiences over the superficiality of virtual interactions.

Nature serves as a profound teacher of the art of simplicity. Observing the natural world's rhythms reveals the elegance and efficiency inherent in simplicity. The beauty of a blooming flower, the simplicity of a flowing stream, and the efficiency of a tree's growth all embody the essence of less being more. Nature operates harmoniously with its surroundings, embracing simplicity in its design and functioning. Emulating the principles of nature in our lives involves recognizing the inherent wisdom of simplicity and aligning our choices with the natural order.

Cultivating a mindset of simplicity does not mean shunning complexity altogether; instead, it involves navigating complexity with a clear and intentional perspective. Life is inherently multifaceted, and challenges, uncertainties, and intricate situations are inevitable. However, a mindset of simplicity equips individuals with the ability to discern what truly matters amidst the complexities of life. It gives them the ability to approach challenges with a focused and uncluttered perspective, allowing them to make decisions that align with their values and contribute to a sense of purpose through their actions.

In conclusion, cultivating a mindset of simplicity is a transformative journey that transcends the confines of minimalism. It is a conscious choice to declutter physical spaces, mental landscapes, and lifestyle choices. Simplicity is a philosophy that encourages intentional living, fostering clarity, purpose, and a deeper connection to the essence of life. By embracing simplicity, individuals can navigate the complexities of the modern world with a sense of calm, authenticity, and a renewed appreciation for the beauty in the uncomplicated and essential aspects of existence.

CHAPTER IV

Energy Independence

Solar Power Basics

Solar power has emerged as a frontrunner in the quest for cleaner and more sustainable energy sources, capturing the imagination of individuals, businesses, and governments alike. At its core, solar power harnesses the abundant and renewable energy emitted by the sun to generate electricity. This technology has witnessed remarkable advancements in recent decades, making solar power an increasingly viable and economically competitive option. Understanding the basics of solar power is essential as we navigate a global transition towards more sustainable energy solutions, seeking to reduce our reliance on finite fossil fuels and mitigate the environmental impacts of traditional energy generation.

The foundation of solar power lies in photovoltaic (PV) cells, commonly known as solar cells, which are the building blocks of solar panels. These cells are made from semiconductor materials, typically silicon, and function by converting sunlight directly into electricity through a process known as the photovoltaic effect. When photons from sunlight strike the surface of the solar cells, they dislodge electrons from the atoms within the semiconductor material, generating an electric current. This direct conversion of the sun into electricity is a fundamental principle that underlies the efficiency and sustainability of solar power systems.

Solar panels, made up of solar cells connected to one another, are the primary structural elements of solar power systems. These panels come in various shapes and sizes, catering to diverse applications ranging from residential rooftops to expansive solar farms. The arrangement of solar cells in panels facilitates the efficient capture of sunlight, maximizing the conversion of solar energy into electricity. Advances in solar panel technology have increased efficiency, durability, and affordability, making solar power installations more accessible to a broader range of consumers.

One of the defining features of solar power is its

decentralization of energy generation. Unlike traditional power plants that rely on centralized generation and distribution systems, solar power systems can be deployed on a distributed scale closer to the point of consumption. This decentralization offers several advantages, including reduced transmission losses, increased grid resilience, and the potential for communities to generate their clean energy. Residential and commercial solar installations, commonly known as rooftop solar, exemplify this decentralized approach, allowing individuals and businesses to produce their electricity and, in some cases, contribute surplus energy back to the grid.

The efficiency of solar panels is a critical consideration in

maximizing the energy output from sunlight. The efficiency of a solar panel refers to its ability to convert sunlight into electricity, typically measured as a percentage of the total sunlight energy that hits the panel. Advances in solar technology have led to improvements in efficiency, with modern solar panels achieving efficiencies ranging from 15% to 22% or more. Higher efficiency panels allow for more excellent electricity production in a given space, making them particularly advantageous for installations with limited space.

Solar power installations can be categorized into two

main types: grid-tied and off-grid systems. Grid-tied systems are connected to the standard electrical grid, allowing users to draw electricity from the grid when solar production is insufficient and feed surplus energy back into the grid when production exceeds demand. These systems often incorporate net metering, a billing arrangement that credits users for the excess electricity they contribute to the grid. In contrast, off-grid systems are designed to operate independently of the grid, relying on energy storage solutions such as batteries to store excess electricity for use during periods of low or no solar production. Off-grid solar power systems are commonly employed in remote or rural areas where access to the grid is limited.

Energy storage is a crucial aspect of solar power systems, addressing the intermittent nature of sunlight. While solar panels create electricity during daylight hours, energy storage options, such as batteries, enable customers to access solar-generated electricity during periods without sunshine. Advances in energy storage technology have led to the development of more efficient and cost-effective batteries, enhancing the reliability and versatility of solar power systems. Energy storage also plays a crucial role in improving grid resilience by providing a buffer against energy demand and supply fluctuations.

The lifecycle of solar panels is an essential consideration in evaluating their overall environmental impact. While solar power is recognized for its green credentials, the manufacturing, use, and disposal of solar panels involve energy and resource inputs. When evaluating the environmental benefits of solar power, one of the most important metrics to consider is the energy payback period, which refers to the time it takes for a solar panel to generate the same amount of energy used in its production. With ongoing improvements in manufacturing processes and recycling initiatives, the environmental impact of solar panels continues to decrease, further solidifying their position as a sustainable energy solution.

Solar power has gained widespread acceptance and support due to its environmental benefits, including reducing greenhouse gas emissions and mitigating climate change. Solar energy systems produce electricity without emitting pollutants, such as carbon dioxide, sulfur dioxide, or nitrogen oxides, associated with conventional fossil fuel-based power generation. Solar power contributes to a cleaner and more sustainable energy mix, aligning with global efforts to transition towards low-carbon and renewable energy sources.

Government incentives and policies play a crucial role in fostering the adoption of solar power. Many countries offer financial incentives, tax credits, and rebates to encourage individuals and businesses to invest in solar installations. Feed-in tariffs, which guarantee a fixed payment for the electricity generated by solar systems, provide additional financial incentives. These policies aim to make solar power more economically attractive and accelerate the transition towards a renewable energy future. The regulatory landscape, advancements in technology, and decreasing costs have contributed to the widespread adoption of solar power globally.

Solar power's versatility extends beyond traditional solar panels. Solar thermal technology harnesses sunlight to generate heat, which can be used for various applications, including space heating, water heating, and industrial processes. Concentrated solar power (CSP) systems use mirrors or lenses to focus sunlight onto a small area, generating high-temperature heat that can be used to produce electricity. These diverse solar technologies cater to different energy needs and offer various options for harnessing the sun's energy.

While solar power has made considerable progress, problems still need to be solved, including intermittent power, land use concerns, and efficient energy storage solutions. Overcoming these challenges requires continued research, innovation, and collaboration between governments, industries, and research institutions. Emerging technologies, such as advanced photovoltaics, innovative materials, and next-generation energy storage, can address these challenges and further enhance the viability of solar power as a mainstream energy source.

In conclusion, solar power is a beacon of hope in the global pursuit of sustainable and clean energy solutions. By harnessing the sun's abundant and renewable energy, solar power systems contribute to reducing environmental impacts, mitigating climate change, and fostering energy independence. Understanding the basics of solar power is essential as we navigate the complexities of transitioning towards a more sustainable energy future. From the science of photovoltaics to the applications of solar energy in various settings, solar power promises a brighter, cleaner, and more sustainable tomorrow. As technology progresses, costs decrease, and worldwide awareness grows, solar power is positioned to play an increasingly critical role in the global energy landscape.

Wind and Hydro Energy

As the world grapples with the challenges of climate change and the depletion of finite energy resources, the quest for sustainable and renewable energy solutions has gained unprecedented momentum. Among the most promising sources of clean energy are wind and hydropower, both of which capitalize on the earth's natural forces to generate electricity. Wind energy harnesses the kinetic energy of moving air, while hydro energy taps into the gravitational potential energy of flowing water. Understanding the concepts, applications, and benefits of these renewable energy sources is vital as societies around the globe aim to shift to a more sustainable and resilient energy landscape.

Wind energy, a cornerstone of the renewable energy revolution, is obtained from the kinetic energy of moving air masses. This energy has been harnessed for centuries, initially for milling grain and later for pumping water. However, it is in the modern period that wind energy has fully come into its own as a significant participant in the global energy mix. Wind turbines, the iconic symbols of wind energy, are comprised of blades that capture the wind's kinetic energy and convert it into rotational energy. A generator is activated as a result of this rotation, which results in the production of electricity that can be incorporated into the power grid.

Onshore and offshore wind farms are the primary installations for large-scale wind energy generation. Onshore wind farms consist of arrays of wind turbines erected on land, often in areas with consistent and robust wind patterns. Offshore wind farms in bodies of water use more substantial and more regular winds found at sea. The advancement of wind turbine technology, with taller towers and larger rotor diameters, has contributed to increasing efficiency and energy generation. Advances in materials, such as lightweight and durable composite materials for turbine blades, enhance the performance and longevity of wind turbines.

The benefits of wind energy are multifaceted. First and foremost, wind power is a clean and renewable energy source that produces minimal greenhouse gas emissions during operation, contributing significantly to efforts to mitigate climate change. Furthermore, wind energy enhances energy security by diversifying the energy mix and reducing reliance on fossil fuels, which are limited in supply. Wind power may also generate employment opportunities and stimulate economic growth, particularly in areas with abundant wind resources. Wind power is becoming an increasingly viable alternative to conventional methods of producing electricity as technological advancements continue to be made, and costs continue to fall.

However, some obstacles must be overcome before wind energy can become widely used. The intermittent nature of wind power, which refers to the fluctuation in wind speeds, presents a challenge to the reliability of wind power. Because of this intermittent nature, it is necessary to implement energy storage solutions or backup power sources to guarantee a steady electricity supply. Other factors that have contributed to opposition to specific wind farm projects include worries about the visual impact of wind turbines, the potential for noise pollution, and the potential for adverse effects on wildlife. Maintaining a healthy equilibrium between the advantages of wind energy and the concerns above calls for meticulous planning, active participation from the community, and the development of innovative technological solutions.

Hydroenergy, another stalwart in the realm of renewable energy, depends on the gravitational potential energy contained within moving water to generate electricity. Utilizing water, a force that is both powerful and dependable, has been something that has been done for centuries to power mills and a variety of industrial processes. In contemporary hydroelectric power generation, large-scale facilities use the kinetic energy of falling or flowing water to turn turbines connected to generators, thereby producing electricity. Two primary types of hydroelectric power can be distinguished from one another: conventional hydropower, which is characterized by the presence of dams and reservoirs, and run-of-river hydropower, which is characterized by the absence of dams and is dependent on the natural flow of rivers.

The construction of dams to create reservoirs, which are used to store water and regulate its release, is typically required for conventional hydropower plants so that they can generate electricity. The water that is released from the reservoir in a controlled manner flows through turbines, which results in the generation of electricity. The stored water in the reservoir serves as energy storage, allowing for flexibility in electricity generation to meet fluctuating demand. Examples of conventional hydropower installations considered iconic include large-scale hydroelectric dams like the Three Gorges Dam in China and the Hoover Dam in the United States.

On the other hand, run-of-river hydropower does not necessitate the construction of large dams or reservoirs. Instead, it generates electricity by turning the natural flow of rivers into a source of energy. In run-of-the-river systems, water is diverted from the river through a canal or penstock, passing through turbines before being returned to the river downstream. Run-of-the-river hydropower plants have a smaller environmental footprint than conventional dams, as they do not alter river ecosystems or require large reservoirs. These installations benefit places with steady river flows but limited possibilities for significant dams.There are numerous and significant benefits associated with hydroenergy. In the same way, wind power is a clean and renewable energy source, hydroelectricity is also a source of energy that produces minimal emissions of greenhouse gases due to its operation. The predictability of river water flow and the ability to regulate reservoir levels contribute to the reliability and stability of hydroelectric power generation. Additionally, hydroenergy provides energy storage in reservoirs, allowing for water storage during periods of low demand and its release during peak demand. Because of this storage capability, the grid's flexibility is increased, and it also helps to maintain grid stability.

Despite its numerous advantages, hydro energy faces challenges and concerns. Building large dams and reservoirs can have significant environmental and social impacts. Several common problems are associated with large-scale hydropower projects. These concerns include changes in water quality, the displacement of communities, and alterations to river ecosystems. In addition, climate change has the potential to influence the availability of water and the flow of rivers, respectively, which may affect the efficiency of hydroelectric facilities. Striking a balance between the benefits and problems of hydro energy needs careful site selection, environmental impact evaluations, and community engagement.

Both wind and hydro energy have made substantial contributions to worldwide electricity generation. The International Energy Agency (IEA) estimates that hydropower was responsible for over sixteen percent of the world's electricity output in 2019, while wind power was responsible for nearly nine percent. With countries increasing their investments in renewable energy and decreasing their reliance on fossil fuels, these percentages are anticipated to continue to rise. Furthermore, improvements in technology and current research continue to better the efficiency and environmental sustainability of both wind and hydro energy.

As the globe accelerates efforts to address climate change and transition to a low-carbon economy, the role of wind and hydroenergy becomes increasingly essential. Each of these sources provides dependable and abundant renewable energy solutions that have the potential to replace electricity generation that is dependent on fossil fuels. The intermittent nature of wind and the site-specific considerations of hydro requires thoughtful planning and integration with other forms of energy generation and storage. A diverse and resilient energy mix that addresses the challenges of climate change and environmental degradation can be achieved through the synergy between wind and hydro energy, in addition to alternative forms of renewable energy.To sum everything up, wind

And hydro energy represents powerful and proven solutions on the journey towards a sustainable, low-carbon energy future. Harnessing the kinetic energy of the wind and the gravitational potential energy of flowing water, these renewable sources offer clean, reliable, and abundant electricity generation options. While hurdles remain, continual technology developments, environmental considerations, and community participation efforts are crucial to harnessing the full potential of wind and hydro energy. By embracing these natural forces, communities can lessen their carbon footprint, improve their energy security, and pave the way for a global energy environment that is more robust and sustainable.

Reducing Energy Consumptiond. Energy Storage Solutions

In the face of escalating energy demand, environmental concerns, and the imperative to combat climate change, the twin challenges of reducing energy consumption and developing effective energy storage solutions have become paramount in the global quest for sustainability. The intertwined nature of these challenges necessitates a holistic approach that combines energy efficiency measures with innovative storage technologies. It is widely acknowledged that reducing consumption and efficiently storing energy is pivotal in developing a resilient and environmentally conscious energy landscape. This is because societies all over the world are working toward the transition to energy systems that are cleaner and more sustainable.

Reducing energy usage is the cornerstone of environmentally responsible energy production and consumption practices. The desire to minimize energy use arises from both environmental and economic factors. The consumption of energy, particularly from non-renewable sources like fossil fuels, contributes to the emission of greenhouse gases, the pollution of the air, and the depletion of resources. Simultaneously, rising energy consumption strains existing energy infrastructure and exacerbates the need for continual development, often requiring more power plants and transmission lines. As a consequence of this, strategies that aim to reduce energy consumption have the potential to reduce the adverse effects on the environment, improve energy security, and generate economic benefits through cost savings.

One of the primary initiatives for lowering energy usage is improving energy efficiency across diverse sectors. Energy-efficient technologies and practices aim to deliver the same or enhanced services using less energy. Regarding the residential sector, this may involve utilizing more energy-efficient appliances, improved insulation, and technologies used in smart homes. Implementing energy-efficient machinery, optimizing processes, and implementing comprehensive energy management systems are all examples of energy efficiency measures that can be implemented in commercial and industrial settings. Governments and organizations worldwide are developing energy efficiency standards, rules, and labeling programs to incentivize and control the implementation of efficient solutions across multiple industries.

The implementation of energy-saving methods is another important factor in the reduction of consumption. These practices entail purposeful efforts to use less energy by adopting behaviors such as turning off lights when not needed, taking public transportation, and limiting waste. To cultivate a culture of conservation, it is essential to conduct public awareness campaigns and educational activities and provide rewards for actions that demonstrate energy efficiency. Building design and urban planning that prioritize energy efficiency also reduce communities' overall energy demand.

Renewable energy sources, such as solar and wind power, are still another approach that could be used to reduce overall energy consumption. Changing from power generation based on fossil fuels to power generation based on renewable sources allows societies to simultaneously reduce their carbon footprint and their reliance on limited resources. Incorporating decentralized renewable energy systems, such as rooftop solar installations and small-scale wind turbines, allows individuals and communities to generate their own clean energy, which further contributes to the reduction of consumption from centralized power grids.

There is a need for efficient energy storage solutions because of the intermittent nature of renewable energy sources, even though lowering energy consumption is essential to ecological sustainability. Using energy storage, supply and demand can be brought into equilibrium, fluctuations in electricity generation can be managed, and a reliable electricity supply can be facilitated. Developing dependable and efficient energy storage technologies is essential for unlocking the full potential of renewable energy and guaranteeing a robust and stable energy infrastructure.

Batteries are among the most widespread types of energy storage. Advances in battery technology, spurred by the increased demand for electric vehicles (EVs) and renewable energy integration, have led to energy density, cycle life, and cost-effectiveness. In particular, lithium-ion batteries have emerged as the most popular technology for use in applications involving stationary energy storage, electric cars, and portable electronic gadgets. Grid-scale energy storage that uses batteries makes it possible to store excess energy during times of high generation, such as when the sun is shining, or the wind is blowing so that it can be used during times of low generation or high demand.

In addition to batteries, a variety of other energy storage solutions contribute to the grid's reliability and stability. Pumped storage hydroelectricity is a form of large-scale energy storage that has been around for a long time and is widely utilized. This approach includes pumping water to an elevated reservoir during periods of low energy demand and releasing it to create power during high demand—compressed air energy storage exploits compressed air stored in underground caves or containers to generate electricity when released. Thermal energy storage keeps excess heat or cold created during off-peak hours to use later in applications requiring heating or cooling.

Innovative technologies that can potentially improve energy storage capacities are receiving attention. Some examples of these technologies include flywheel energy storage, supercapacitors, and enhanced thermal storage systems. In addition to contributing to the overall dependability and performance of energy storage systems, these technologies offer several benefits, including high efficiency, short response times, and long cycle lifetimes.

Integrating intelligent grids and demand response programs further enhances the effectiveness of energy storage solutions. The operation of the electricity grid can be improved by using smart grids, which use advanced communication and control technologies. They make it possible to monitor energy consumption in real-time, improve grid stability, and make it easier to integrate renewable energy sources without any disruptions. Customers are incentivized to alter their power consumption in response to the conditions of the grid through demand response programs. This results in a reduction in peak demand and an improvement in the overall reliability of the grid.

Although progress has been achieved in energy storage technology, there are still obstacles to be faced. Some energy storage systems can be prohibitively expensive, particularly for large-scale applications, limiting their general adoption. Ongoing research and development efforts are being made to increase the efficiency of energy storage technologies while simultaneously lowering their costs. In addition, resolving environmental concerns related to the production and disposal of particular types of batteries is a goal for a more sustainable future in terms of energy.

Integrating energy efficiency measures with adequate energy storage technology is a comprehensive and synergistic strategy for achieving a sustainable and resilient energy landscape. By lowering overall energy usage through efficiency improvements and conservation practices

societies can lower their environmental impact,

minimize the need for new energy infrastructure, and realize economic savings. While this is happening, modern energy storage technology makes it possible to include renewable energy sources, improves grid resilience, and paves the way for a more sustainable and decentralized energy system.

When it comes to promoting energy efficiency and

storage, the government's policies and incentives play a significant role. Businesses and individuals are encouraged to invest in sustainable energy solutions by providing financial incentives, subsidies, and regulatory frameworks that encourage energy-efficient practices and the development of energy storage projects. Furthermore, to drive innovation and accelerate the adoption of cutting-edge technologies in the energy sector, it is vital to have robust research and development programs, collaboration between the public and private sectors, and international cooperation.

The reduction of energy consumption and the

development of efficient technologies for energy storage are, in conclusion, essential components of an energy future that is both sustainable and robust. Both of these challenges are inextricably linked, and addressing them simultaneously provides a holistic approach to mitigating the adverse effects of energy generation on the environment, improving energy security, and fostering economic growth. As communities worldwide seek to fulfill the growing demand for energy while mitigating climate change, a systematic and coordinated push toward energy efficiency and enhanced energy storage is needed. Such concerted initiatives can pave the road for a more sustainable, reliable, and ecologically sensitive energy landscape.

CHAPTER V

Water Self-Sufficiency

Rainwater Harvesting

Water scarcity is an escalating global concern exacerbated by climate change, population growth, and inefficient water usage. When confronted with this dilemma, it is necessary to find inventive and sustainable solutions to guarantee that future generations will have access to clean water. The technique of rainwater harvesting, which involves collecting and storing rainwater for a variety of purposes, is one of these solutions that is gaining popularity. The concept of rainwater gathering, as well as its methods, benefits, and obstacles, are investigated in this section. The focus is placed on the potential of rainwater harvesting as an essential instrument in managing sustainable water resources.

The method of collecting rainwater, which dates back

hundreds of years, has been rediscovered and rethought to satisfy the water requirements of the present era. The process begins with collecting rainfall from surfaces, rooftops, or catchment areas and storing the rainwater in tanks, reservoirs, or underground structures. Consequently, this rainwater that has been collected can be utilized for a variety of purposes, including domestic, agricultural, industrial, and environmental purposes, thereby reducing reliance on traditional water sources.

One of the most common approaches to collecting

rainwater is known as rooftop harvesting, which involves collecting rainwater from the balconies and rooftops of buildings. Water collecting can be accomplished in a reasonably straightforward and economical manner through the utilization of gutters and downspouts, which direct water drainage into storage tanks. Surface runoff harvesting is another approach that can be utilized. This technique involves the collection of rainwater from open ground or paved surfaces and its subsequent transfer into storage. Therefore, rainwater harvesting is a versatile option that can be utilized to meet a wide range of water requirements because both methods may be applied on various scales, ranging from individual residences to large-scale industrial complexes.

Collecting rainwater has several advantages, including the fact that it helps with water management in various ways, including the environment, the economy, and society. In the first place, it lessens the burden placed on conventional water sources, such as rivers and groundwater, which helps prevent the depletion of these essential resources. This component of conservation is necessary in locations experiencing the detrimental effects of climate change or water scarcity, both of which are areas in which sustainable water management methods are of the utmost importance.

Adopting rainwater harvesting can lead to significant cost savings for individuals, communities, and industries. Using rainwater collected from the environment, homeowners can reduce their dependence on municipal water supplies, resulting in lower water bills. Similarly, businesses can optimize their water consumption, cutting water treatment and procurement costs. Moreover, rainwater collection can bolster agricultural resilience by providing an alternative water source for irrigation, which is crucial for maintaining crop yield in drought-prone or arid areas.

By embracing rainwater collection, communities gain the power to become self-sufficient in meeting their water requirements, a fundamental human right. This method can be a lifeline in rural areas where traditional water delivery infrastructure may lack or nonexistent, ensuring access to a local and reliable water source.

However, despite the enormous number of advantages it offers, rainwater harvesting is confronted with a number of obstacles that must be overcome before it can achieve broad adoption. One of the most major challenges is the unpredictable nature of the patterns of rainfall. Those areas that are having little or unpredictable rainfall may find it difficult to rely simply on rainwater collection, which may need the use of other water sources or more modern techniques for water storage and conservation. Even though there are long-term economic benefits connected with rainwater harvesting systems, the initial costs of building these systems may discourage some people or groups from initiating the process. To overcome these obstacles, it may be helpful to make efforts to either promote awareness or provide financial incentives.

Moreover, the quality of the rainwater that has been captured needs to be appropriately regulated to guarantee that it satisfies the safety standards for a variety of applications. The quality of the water can be compromised by contaminants from rooftops, storage tanks, or catchment surfaces, which necessitates proper filtering and treatment procedures. Maintenance of harvesting systems should be performed regularly to prevent the accumulation of debris, algae, or bacteria that could have an impact on the quality of the water over time.

In conclusion, rainwater harvesting is a method of water management that is both sustainable and innovative, and it offers a wide range of benefits to individuals, communities, and the environment. Such approaches are becoming increasingly necessary as the water situation on a worldwide scale becomes more severe. Governments, communities, and individuals need to work together to overcome the problems connected with rainwater collection and promote its incorporation into mainstream water resource management policies. We can ensure that future generations will have access to a more sustainable and abundant water supply if we adopt this time-honored method and give it a contemporary twist.

Efficient Water Usage

Water, a resource that is both limited and indispensable, is at the center of the difficulties that are associated with global sustainability. The optimal utilization of water is becoming increasingly crucial for the well-being of the environment, the economy, and society as the world population continues to increase and climate change continues to alter precipitation patterns. This section investigates the relevance of energy-efficient water usage, the difficulties that must be overcome to achieve it, and the sustainable solutions that may be implemented to address the impending water crisis.

To effectively use water, it is necessary to use discretion

and responsibility in administering water resources to fulfill both present and future requirements without jeopardizing the capacity of ecosystems to sustain life. It involves a wide range of operations, including optimizing agricultural irrigation systems, implementing sophisticated industrial processes, and reducing water waste in residential settings. It is impossible to emphasize the significance of water conservation, especially in light of the growing strain that is being placed on water supplies all across the world.

The agricultural sector, a significant consumer of water,

is at the forefront of the challenge of managing water usage efficiently. Traditional irrigation techniques, such as flood irrigation, frequently lead to significant water waste due to evaporation, runoff, and inefficient water distribution throughout the irrigation system. To achieve the highest possible level of water efficiency in agricultural production, it is essential to transition to precision irrigation technologies, such as sprinkler or drip irrigation systems. Not only do these technologies help preserve water, but they also contribute to enhancements in crop yields and optimization of resource utilization, promoting sustainability in the food production industry.

Regarding water use, efficiency is equally important in metropolitan areas with a higher concentration of water demand. To reduce the amount of water consumers consume, execute methods such as installing water-efficient appliances, reconstructing leaking infrastructure, and developing intelligent water management systems. The cultivation of a culture of conservation within communities can be further increased by implementing public awareness campaigns and educational programs that promote responsible water usage habits.

One of the significant contributors to water consumption is the industrial sector; therefore, the sustainability of the industrial sector needs to maximize water utilization in its processes. Additionally, the implementation of water-efficient technology, in conjunction with the recycling and reuse of water within industrial operations, has the potential to lessen the overall water footprint of the sector significantly. By using closed-loop systems and efficient cooling technologies, industries can reduce their influence on local water supplies, contributing to the preservation of the environment and saving money at the same time.

On the other hand, the utilization of water in an efficient manner has its challenges. The general public's need for more awareness and comprehension of the problems associated with water scarcity is one of the most significant obstacles encountered. Many people and groups take water availability seriously, resulting in wasteful habits and disregarding various conservation measures. It is vital to raise awareness through education, outreach programs, and media campaigns to establish a sense of responsibility and foster a general commitment to efficient water usage.

An additional obstacle is that many places have water infrastructure that needs to be updated and improved. Significant amounts of water are lost before it reaches the consumers due to leaking pipes and distribution systems not operating efficiently. It is necessary to invest in the renovation and maintenance of water infrastructure to cut down on water losses and guarantee that water is delivered to end-users efficiently. Collaboration between governments, utilities, and private groups is required to overcome these infrastructure difficulties and invest in intelligent technology that will effectively monitor and manage water distribution networks.

The proper management of water resources is made much more difficult by the effects of climate variation. Alterations in the patterns of precipitation, a rise in the frequency of extreme weather events, and temperature changes all impact the availability and distribution of water. More frequent and severe droughts or floods are occurring in specific locations, which means that water shortage is becoming an issue that is more immediate and important. Adaptive techniques are crucial components When it comes to effectively using water in the face of climate change. These strategies include the creation of climate-adaptable agricultural practices, water storage infrastructure, and water supply systems that are resilient to harsh weather conditions.

Sustainable solutions are essential components of solving the issues related to water efficiency. The encouragement of water recycling and reuse is one option that can be implemented. It is possible to use wastewater treated for uses that do not include drinking water, such as irrigation, industrial processes, or even certain activities in the home. By implementing decentralized wastewater treatment systems, it is possible to improve water availability in the local area and lessen the burden placed on centralized treatment plants.

Water quality maintenance and water flow regulation are significantly aided by implementing nature-based solutions, such as the restoration of watersheds and wetland areas. Ecosystems in good health serve as natural filters, removing contaminants from water and recharging aquifers. Contributing to the overall health of water sources, conservation activities focused on maintaining and restoring these ecosystems contribute to the overall health of water sources, providing a sustainable supply for both humans and the environment.

One such method that contributes to sustainability is water-sensitive urban design. To accomplish this, water management must be incorporated into urban planning. This includes incorporating rain gardens, permeable pavements, and green roofs to collect and manage rainwater. Combining water sensitivity into urban development has many benefits, including reducing stormwater runoff, enhancing groundwater recharge, and mitigating the urban heat island effect. These designs demonstrate the versatility of these benefits.

The development of new technologies is also an essential component in the process of achieving optimal water utilization. This can be accomplished by using sophisticated sensors, data analytics, and artificial intelligence to monitor water consumption, identify leaks, and improve water distribution systems. Irrigation systems equipped with weather data and sensors that measure soil moisture allow for precise and automatic regulation of irrigation, reducing the amount of water wasted in agricultural settings. By incorporating technology into water management, stakeholders are provided with information in real-time, enabling them to make more informed decisions on implementing sustainable water usage guidelines.

In conclusion, efficiently utilizing water is a requirement and a responsibility that individuals, communities, companies, and governments must collectively accept. A comprehensive and coordinated strategy is required to address the difficulties related to declining water supplies, deteriorating infrastructure, and climate change. Through the dissemination of information, the investment in infrastructure, and the implementation of sustainable solutions, we may work toward a future in which water is utilized responsibly, safeguarding the health and happiness of contemporary and future generations. It is only through a concentrated effort and a commitment to change that we will be able to successfully navigate the complicated waters of efficient water usage and ensure a water future that is both sustainable and resilient.

Natural Filtration Methods

Access to clean and safe drinking water is a fundamental human right, yet millions worldwide face waterborne diseases from contaminated water sources. Using natural filtration techniques for water purification has garnered much interest due to the search for environmentally acceptable and sustainable solutions. Since the beginning of time, nature, with all of its complex ecosystems and activities, has motivated the development of novel approaches. This section aims to investigate the many natural filtration systems, their mechanics, and the potential that these approaches hold for revolutionizing water purification in a world that is struggling with issues related to water quality.

Using soil and sediments as filtering media is a common and widely used natural filtration technology. Percolating water through soil functions as a biological filter, eliminating pollutants and toxins from the water as it passes through the soil. This process is analogous to the earth's natural water purification system, in which precipitation seeps into the ground, passes through biological filtration, and ultimately replenishes groundwater aquifers. The removal of suspended particles, bacteria, and certain chemicals can be accomplished through soil-based filtration, which is a straightforward and highly effective way to enhance water quality.

In addition to being referred to as the "kidneys of the earth," wetland ecosystems are excellent examples of natural filtration devices. These habitats, distinguished by standing water and a wide range of plants, are critical in water purification. Both physically and biologically, wetland ecosystems serve as filters, capturing sediments and pollutants while fostering the growth of microbes responsible for the breakdown of many toxic compounds. Constructed wetlands, which are meant to emulate the natural processes of wetland filtration, have been successfully adopted for wastewater treatment and stormwater management. This demonstrates the potential for exploiting the inherent capabilities of wetland ecosystems.

Forests also make a substantial contribution to the natural filtration of water. As a natural sponge, the intricate root systems of trees and the forest floor filter rainwater, allowing it to percolate gently into the earth. This process is known as "percolation." Not only does this procedure help to replenish groundwater, but it also contributes to the reduction of surface runoff, the prevention of soil erosion, and the preservation of healthy water quality. Forestry watersheds are necessary to protect the quality of rivers and streams because they act as natural barriers against pollutants and toxins.

Peat, wood, and coconut shells are all-natural supplies that can produce activated carbon, another effective biological filtration media. Activated carbon, which is well-known for its remarkable adsorption characteristics, can attract and bind to pollutants such as organic molecules, chemicals, and some heavy metals from the environment. Because of this, activated carbon is a substance frequently utilized in water treatment procedures, either in the form of filters or as a powdered addition. An environmentally beneficial alternative to synthetic filtration materials is provided by using activated carbon derived from plants, which is natural. This accords with the ideals of sustainability.

Water hyacinths and lilies are examples of aquatic plants carrying a dual function in natural water filtering. The extensive root systems of these plants serve as a physical barrier, capturing sediments and suspended particles. Additionally, the plants themselves contribute to the uptake of nutrients and the biological filtering of water. For water treatment in ponds and lakes, floating islands seeded with aquatic vegetation have been utilized in select places as an economical and environmentally friendly solution. To improve water quality, these natural systems use the mutually beneficial relationship between plants and water.

On the other hand, oysters and other shellfish are effective natural water cleansers in aquatic areas, in addition to their use in terrestrial ecosystems. Through absorbing and removing pollutants from the water, oyster reefs perform the function of natural filters. They remove particles, bacteria, and excess nutrients from vast quantities of water through the process of filtering, which contributes to an improvement in the purity and quality of the water. As a nature-based option for improving water filtration and restoring the health of estuarine and coastal ecosystems, oyster restoration projects have gained interest as a potential alternative.

The processes of filtration that occur in nature extend to the world of microbes, where specific bacteria and algae make significant contributions to water purification. Biologically active sand filters utilize the natural microbial communities in the sand to remove pathogens and break down organic materials. These filters use the natural self-purification capabilities of microorganisms, which are frequently utilized in decentralized water treatment systems. Through the process of absorbing nutrients and creating oxygen, algae, and more specifically certain species of microalgae and macroalgae, contribute to the purification of water sources. It has been demonstrated that the cultivation of algae in water treatment systems has the potential to remove nutrients and improve the overall quality of the water.

Even though these natural filtration technologies hold great potential, putting them into practice is challenging. The effectiveness of biological filtering processes can be affected by various factors, including ambient conditions, seasonal fluctuations, and the particular properties of the water source. It is necessary to engage in thorough planning and modification to scale up these procedures to satisfy the requirements of huge populations or industrial environments. A further risk that needs to be addressed in the design and maintenance of natural filtration systems is the possibility of contaminants that have been captured being released back into the environment while some filtration media is regenerated.

It is necessary to take a holistic and integrated strategy to include natural filtering techniques in contemporary water treatment solutions successfully. Utilizing these techniques with traditional water treatment technologies can improve efficiency and resilience. Furthermore, to fully capitalize on the advantages of natural filtration, it is necessary to have a comprehensive awareness of the ecosystems and hydrological cycles of the area, as well as the particular obstacles that are peculiar to each place.

In conclusion, natural filtering techniques offer a viable path for solving water quality concerns in a manner that is both sustainable and harmonious. It is possible to harness the inherent capabilities of soil, wetlands, forests, aquatic plants, and microbial communities to purify water. This can be accomplished by pulling inspiration from the complex processes that occur in ecosystems. Incorporating these natural filtering systems into our water management practices provides a glimmer of hope for a future in which clean and safe water is available to everyone. This is particularly relevant because the world struggles with rising water stress and pollution. We can pave the way for a water future that is both healthier and more sustainable if we work together to combine the knowledge that nature has to offer with the inventiveness of humans.

Emergency Water Sources

Water is an indispensable resource for sustaining life, yet emergencies and disasters can disrupt regular water supplies, leaving communities vulnerable to dehydration, waterborne diseases, and many challenges. In times of disaster, having access to emergency water sources that are both safe and reliable becomes of the utmost importance. This section aims to investigate the numerous sources of emergency water, the significance of these sources during times of disaster, and the techniques necessary to ensure communities' resilience in the face of restricted water supplies.

There is the potential for natural disasters such as earthquakes, hurricanes, floods, and droughts to have a significant influence on water infrastructure, causing conventional water sources to become contaminated or depleted. In circumstances as terrible as these, the capacity to recognize and make use of sources of emergency water becomes an essential component of disaster preparedness and response. A significant supply of water for emergencies is groundwater. Wells, boreholes, and springs draw water from underground aquifers, making them a dependable and reasonably safe water source in an emergency. Wells created and managed correctly are precious assets because they provide a means of survival if surface water becomes contaminated or inaccessible.

Even though surface water is susceptible to pollution during times of crisis, it continues to be an essential source of water for emergencies. When outfitted with portable water purifying technologies, rivers, lakes, and ponds can temporarily supply water. This is especially true when equipped with these technologies. It is common practice for emergency response teams to deploy mobile water treatment units to cleanse vast quantities of surface water rapidly. This ensures that affected populations have access to a source of water that is both quick and easily accessible. On the other hand, it is necessary to carry out exhaustive water quality evaluations to reduce the potential health hazards related to probable contaminants.

Rainwater harvesting emerges as a viable and sustainable emergency water source that becomes especially important in prolonged emergencies or droughts. Providing communities with a decentralized and independent water supply can be accomplished by collecting rainwater from rooftops and other surfaces and storing it in containers. Rainwater harvesting systems that are appropriately managed and equipped with filtration and purification processes have the potential to provide a dependable source of clean water in situations where traditional sources of water are disrupted.

Desalination has the potential to be an essential component in the provision of emergency water in coastal areas. To make seawater drinkable, desalination methods, such as reverse osmosis, remove salt and other contaminants from the water. Desalination is an essential choice during times of emergency when access to fresh water is severely limited. Even though it is energy-intensive and frequently expensive, desalination is a need. It has been demonstrated that mobile desalination units are an efficient means of giving vital assistance to coastal towns that natural catastrophes have impacted.

The needs of displaced people now housed in temporary shelters must be considered as part of efforts to secure access to emergency water sources. In humanitarian interventions, portable water purifying technologies, water trucking, and distribution networks become critical components. Hygiene and sanitation facilities need to be incorporated into emergency water supply schemes to minimize the spread of waterborne infections, which are an extra hazard during times of crisis.

On the other hand, the efficient usage of emergency water sources is fraught with many challenges. Several factors, including damage to infrastructure, logistical restrictions, and the sheer magnitude of catastrophes, frequently hamper the timely deployment of water supply solutions. In addition, there is a continual concern regarding the water quality from emergency sources. Contamination hazards, insufficient purification, and the possibility of spreading diseases transmitted through water are all daunting obstacles that call for careful planning and prompt action with immediate consequences. In order to protect the health of the general public, it is essential to find a middle ground between the urgency surrounding water availability and the adoption of stringent water quality regulations.

Innovative technologies play a crucial role when it comes to solving these difficulties and improving the resilience of emergency water delivery systems. Solar-powered water purifying machines, for example, provide a potentially sustainable alternative, particularly in areas that receive significant sunlight. These devices, which are highly portable and compact, have the potential to supply communities with a dependable source of clean water that is powered by renewable energy. Additionally, developments in nanotechnology and filtration materials help create practical, compact, and cost-effective water purification systems. These devices are also well-suited for use in emergencies.

Participation from the community and the development of their capabilities are essential elements of efficient emergency water supply emergency planning. The empowerment of local communities to identify and manage emergency water sources, the education of these communities on water quality testing, and the promotion of sustainable water use practices all contribute to the empowerment of local communities to create resilience at the grassroots level. It is possible to provide a prompt and efficient reaction during times of crisis by offering individuals on emergency response teams training on how to operate water treatment infrastructure.

It is necessary to have legal and policy frameworks in

place to construct a solid foundation for emergency water supply planning. Legislation that enables the rapid deployment of emergency water sources and ensures the protection of these sources from contamination is something that governments need to pass. To develop an approach to emergency water supply management that is both comprehensive and coordinated, governmental agencies, non-governmental groups, and the commercial sector need to work together.

In addition, measures for crisis management need to

consider the influence that climate change will have on the supply of water and the patterns of extreme weather phenomena. Because of the growing frequency and severity of natural catastrophes, it is necessary to implement adaptive solutions that consider the shifting dynamics of water supplies. Regarding emergency water supply planning, incorporating climate resilience involves predicting shifts in precipitation patterns, rising temperatures, and the possibility of more violent storms. This helps to ensure that communities are ready to face developing issues.

In the event of an emergency, the importance of

international collaboration in the provision of water cannot be stressed. Because disasters frequently occur across national boundaries, it is necessary to work together to provide aid and resources. When delivering impacted nations with financial assistance, technical expertise, and logistical support to develop and maintain emergency water supply systems, international organizations, donor countries, and humanitarian agencies play a crucial role in assisting.

Providing emergency water sources is essential to catastrophe resilience and response methods. Because access to clean water is inextricably tied to public health, sanitation, and overall well-being, the capacity to secure safe and reliable water during times of emergency is a matter of life and death. Identifying, developing, and maintaining emergency water sources requires collaboration between governments, communities, and organizations. This collaboration should incorporate innovative technology, community empowerment, and climate resilience into comprehensive, well-coordinated policies. Since we are facing a future that will be characterized by an increase in the number of disasters that are caused by climate change, the creation of emergency water supply systems that are robust becomes not only a requirement but also a demonstration of our dedication to protecting the well-being of communities all over the world.

CHAPTER VI

Growing Your Own Food

Sustainable Agriculture Practices

Sustainable agriculture practices have emerged as a transformative force, offering a holistic approach to food production that harmonizes with ecological systems and addresses the pressing challenges of climate change, resource depletion, and environmental degradation. In a world struggling to understand the intricate relationship between food security, ecological sustainability, and economic viability, sustainable agriculture is a possible solution. Within this section's scope, sustainable agriculture's essence is investigated, including its fundamental principles, advantages, and difficulties, as well as the crucial part it plays in forming a resilient and nourished future.

The fundamental goal of sustainable agriculture is to cultivate food in a way that protects and improves the health of the land, reduces the adverse effects on the environment, and ensures that farmers continue to be economically viable. One of the most critical aspects of these practices is acknowledging agriculture as an essential component of the larger ecosystem. This recognition acknowledges the interconnectedness of the health of the soil, the water supplies, the biodiversity, and the well-being of agricultural communities, respectively. Sustainable agriculture's goal is to encourage regenerative techniques that revitalize the natural resources that agriculture relies on. This is accomplished by adopting a long-term view.

Cover cropping and crop rotation are two strategies that are core concepts in sustainable agriculture. These methods emphasize the significance of preserving the fertility and structure of the soil. Cover crops, which include legumes and grasses, prevent the soil from being eroded, prevent the growth of weeds, and increase the availability of nutrients by fixing nitrogen. Through crop rotation, plant species are diversified over time, lowering the danger of diseases and pests while promoting balanced nutrient cycles. These methods not only improve the soil's health but also make crops more resistant to the effects of shifting environmental conditions.

"agroforestry" refers to innovative and sustainable agriculture incorporating trees and shrubs into conventional farming methods. Enhanced biodiversity, improved soil structure, and increased water-use efficiency are just some of the benefits that can be experienced with the implementation of this multi-dimensional strategy. Agroforestry systems contribute to the development of agricultural ecosystems that are more robust and resilient by providing shade, windbreaks, and habitat for creatures that are useful to agriculture. Additionally, the use of trees in agricultural practices helps to sequester carbon, which in turn reduces the influence that agriculture has on temperature and climate change.

Conservation tillage is yet another critical ecologically responsible agricultural strategy that poses a challenge to traditional plowing techniques. Through the reduction of soil disturbance, conservation tillage helps maintain the soil's structure, limit the amount of erosion that occurs, and improve water retention. This strategy helps preserve vital topsoil and leads to lower energy inputs and reduced greenhouse gas emissions related to traditional methods of tilling the soil.

Considering the growing strain that is being placed on water resources, water management is an essential component of developing sustainable agricultural practices. Farmers can maximize their water use through precision irrigation technology such as drip or sprinkler systems, which supply water precisely to the root zone of their growing crops. An old practice that has been reinvigorated, rainwater harvesting entails collecting and storing rainwater for agricultural use, hence reducing reliance on conventional water sources. Sustainable water management helps preserve this valuable resource but also helps reduce the adverse effects of agricultural runoff on the surrounding environment.

One of the most essential pillars of sustainable agriculture is organic farming, which emphasizes natural processes, biodiversity, and the absence of synthetic inputs. By avoiding synthetic pesticides and fertilizers and instead relying on organic alternatives, organic farming techniques contribute to the development of more robust ecosystems and lessen the impact of agriculture on the environment. Composting, green manure, and biological pest management are some of the activities that organic farming systems implement to nurture the soil and help encourage sustainable crop production. Organic farming systems place a priority on the health of the soil.

In addition, sustainable agriculture promotes the use of agroecological concepts, which emphasizes the incorporation of ecological understandings into agricultural practices. The field of agroecology acknowledges the complex interrelationships between crops, pests, and beneficial species. This approach promotes the development of farming practices that are in tune with the natural environment. This all-encompassing strategy goes beyond the immediate objective of optimizing yields to construct resilient agricultural ecosystems that can withstand the challenge of time.

Sustainable agriculture has many advantages but is full of possible difficulties. It is necessary to make a mental change, acquire new knowledge, and frequently make substantial initial investments to transition from conventional to sustainable practices. Farmers can encounter challenges such as restricted access to environmentally friendly inputs, financial resources, and professional assistance. The immediate economic benefits associated with conventional agriculture, in conjunction with market arrangements that promote high-input, monoculture systems, have the potential to impede the broad adoption of sustainable methods. Politicians, researchers, farmers, and consumers must work together to bridge these gaps and create an environment conducive to sustainable agriculture.

In addition, taking a systems-thinking approach is necessary because sustainable agriculture is characterized by its intricate and interdependent nature. The operation of agroecological systems is based on a collection of interconnected concepts that, when applied collectively, produce favorable results. The full potential of sustainable agriculture may not be realized if specific methods are used in isolation. Comprehensive solutions that incorporate a variety of sustainable practices and are customized to the particular settings and conditions of the local area give a more nuanced and successful approach to the construction of agricultural systems that are resilient and sustainable.

Sustainable agriculture has positive effects on the environment, society, and the economy. Sustainable agricultural techniques contribute to long-term food security by protecting the fertility of the land. This helps to ensure that future generations will be able to meet or exceed their nutritional requirements. The preservation of genetic diversity is an essential resource in the face of shifting environmental conditions. Promoting biodiversity in agroecosystems strengthens resistance to diseases and pests and protects and preserves genetic diversity. Sustainable agricultural practices, such as organic farming, frequently enhance soil health. This, in turn, helps cultivate a thriving microbial population, which contributes to the cycling of nutrients and the general equilibrium of the ecosystem.

In terms of the economy, sustainable agriculture can

improve the resiliency of farmers and their current means of subsistence. Agroecosystems that are both diverse and robust are less likely to be affected by the dangers that are associated with monoculture systems, such as the occurrence of pest outbreaks or the failure of crops. Using synthetic pesticides and fertilizers can be minimized by using sustainable practices, which can result in lower input costs (input costs). Furthermore, as consumers' awareness and the demand for food that is produced sustainably continues to rise, farmers who embrace sustainable agriculture may discover new market opportunities and premium prices for their products.

Sustainable agriculture is vital in the fight against

climate change when viewed from the broader perspective of global concerns. Extreme weather events, altering precipitation patterns, and rising temperatures are some of the risks that agriculture faces due to climate change. Agriculture is both a contributor to climate change and a sufferer. Sustainable agricultural techniques, which emphasize resilience, carbon sequestration, and adaptation, provide a strategy that is both practicable and effective in mitigating the consequences of climate change on food production.

The interconnected crises of climate change, loss of

biodiversity, and environmental degradation highlight the critical need to adopt sustainable agricultural methods as quickly as possible within the farming sector. To promote the transition to sustainable agriculture, governments, agricultural organizations, and the private sector need to work together to create policies conducive to the transition, the provision of financial incentives, and the dissemination of knowledge. It is essential to implement education and outreach initiatives to increase awareness among farmers and customers alike, thereby promoting a deeper understanding of the practices and advantages connected with sustainable agriculture.

In conclusion, sustainable agriculture is equivalent to a paradigm change in our approach to food production since it is by the values of environmental stewardship, social equality, and economic viability. Because the world's population is still expanding and the effects of climate change are becoming more severe, the necessity of transitioning to sustainable agriculture is becoming more apparent than ever. Communities can cultivate resilient food systems that nourish the present and maintain the future if they embrace diverse and regenerative activities on the part of their members. Because of our collective dedication to sustainable agriculture, we can develop a world in which the earth's bounties can satisfy the needs of all people while remaining in peace with the natural environment.

Permaculture Principles

Permaculture, coined by Bill Mollison and David Holmgren in the 1970s, represents a holistic approach to designing sustainable and regenerative systems that mimic natural ecosystems. Permaculture is an approach to environmental management that is founded on the ideas of observation, careful planning, and ecological stewardship. Its goal is to build resilient, productive, and harmonious habitats. An examination of the fundamental concepts of permaculture, its applications, and the tremendous influence that these ideas may have on sustainable agriculture, land management, and community development is presented in this section.

Permaculture is based on "Observation and Interaction," which means "observation and interaction." Permaculturists highlight the significance of studying a particular location's natural patterns, climate, and ecology before employing any design. This is done before any design is implemented. By paying close attention to the interactions within an ecosystem, practitioners can obtain insights into how the various components work together. Permaculture design is informed by this idea, which encourages a profound connection with the land and cultivates an awareness that permeates every facet of the design process. It is important to note that observation is not a one-time event but a continuous process that enables adaptive management to be implemented as the system develops.

In permaculture, the concept of "Catch and Store Energy" is an essential idea emphasizing the practical usage of existing natural resources. Permaculture designs aim to gather and store energy in various forms, including, but not limited to, sunlight and water. Rainwater harvesting systems, for example, are designed to collect and store rainwater for later use. This not only ensures a stable water supply but also reduces reliance on sources that are external to the system. Additionally, passive solar design in architecture is a method of capturing and storing solar energy, which results in the creation of living spaces that are energy-efficient and harmonious with the nature around them.

"Obtain a Yield" encapsulates the pragmatic spirit underpinning permaculture. Even though permaculture designs are primarily concerned with long-term sustainability, they are also meant to deliver beneficial outcomes. Permaculturists emphasize the significance of obtaining a yield as an essential component of sustainable design. This is true whether the cultivation of food, the production of renewable energy, or the creation of habitat for wildlife is being considered. This theory demonstrates that sustainability and abundance are not mutually exclusive concepts, as they stimulate the development of productive and regenerative systems.

The phrase "Apply Self-Regulation and Accept Feedback" highlights the importance of ongoing learning and adaptation. There is no such thing as a static design in permaculture; instead, it develops in response to shifting conditions and feedback from the system. By adhering to this approach, practitioners are encouraged to evaluate the results of their designs, gain knowledge from their successes and mistakes, and make adjustments accordingly. It cultivates an attitude of humility, acknowledging that nature gives valuable feedback and that human intervention should be aligned with natural processes rather than against them.

The phrase "Use and Value Renewable Resources and Services" highlights the significance of prioritizing abundant and renewable resources over other resources. Design principles that adhere to permaculture principles avoid relying on limited resources and instead prioritize those that can be naturally regenerated. This idea can be used in methods such as agroforestry, in which trees provide a variety of functions, including the cycling of nutrients, the creation of windbreaks, and the provision of habitat, all while continuously renewing themselves. Permaculture encourages the development of sustainable systems capable of withstanding the test of time by aligning themselves with renewable resources.

The permaculture philosophy, "Produce No Waste," incorporates eliminating waste while maximizing efficiency. It is possible for waste from one element to become a resource of another component in natural ecosystems. Using methods such as reducing, reusing, and recycling resources, permaculture designs aim to simulate the closed-loop system described above. Composting, for instance, is a process that converts organic waste into compost that is rich in nutrients and increases the richness of the soil. By adhering to the idea of "Produce No Waste," permaculturists contribute to a more sustainable and regenerative resource utilization cycle.

"Design from Patterns to Details" is a guide that assists practitioners of permaculture in the process of developing designs that are both comprehensive and integrated. Initially, designers can concentrate on the exact elements of a system when they have identified and comprehended the overarching patterns of the system. Instead of focusing on individual components, this idea encourages taking a holistic approach that considers the connections between different pieces. Design professionals are encouraged to search for patterns in the natural world and to take their cues from the efficiencies that may be discovered in ecosystems.

The concept of "Integrate Rather Than Segregate"

opposes the traditional idea of components being separated from one another and instead promotes the integration of these components. Diversity is cherished in natural systems, and the various components of these systems work together synergistically. This notion is adhered to by permaculture designs, which incorporate plants, animals, and structures to establish mutually beneficial connections. An excellent example is companion planting, including various plant species to improve nutrient cycling and pest management. Through applying this principle, resilient and autonomous systems that derive their power from diversity are fostered.

The "Use Small and Slow Solutions" approach to

problem-solving encourages a systematic and progressive approach. Instead of adopting interventions on a big scale, permaculturists prefer to implement tiny, achievable solutions that allow for thorough observation and adjustment. This theory is consistent with the notion that gradual and incremental improvements are more likely to be sustainably implemented and successful over time. This enables practitioners to begin on a small scale, gain knowledge from the results, and modify their techniques over time.

The theory known as "Use and Value Diversity"

acknowledges diversity's inherent power and strives to incorporate it into permaculture designs. The resilience and productivity of ecosystems are influenced by biodiversity, including above-ground and below-ground species. Those practicing permaculturists accept a wide variety of plant and animal species and advocate for polycultures rather than monocultures to improve stability and reduce susceptibility to diseases and pests. This notion encompasses not just biological diversity but also diversity in design methods, which helps stimulate creativity and adaptability while promoting diversity.

It is acknowledged in the phrase "Use Edges and Value the Marginal" that the margins, which are the points where distinct ecosystems or elements intersect, frequently include chances that are one of a kind in terms of productivity and diversity. Designs that adhere to permaculture principles purposefully include and seek to utilize the possibilities of these edges. Creating a "food forest" at the edge of a garden, for example, uses the specific conditions present there, allowing for the cultivation of a variety of plants that can thrive in both shade and sunlight. To maximize the utilization of space and resources, permaculturists place a high value on the marginal.

Finally, "Creatively Use and Respond to Change" emphasizes the necessity of accepting change as an intrinsic component of the design process and that change is unavoidable. Designs based on permaculture can anticipate and adjust to shifting conditions, whether those variables are brought about by natural ecological succession, fluctuations in climate, or other reasons. Through this principle, practitioners are encouraged to regard change not as a barrier but as an opportunity for creative adaptation and progress.

When taken as a whole, these permaculture principles constitute a framework that may be utilized for designing resilient, regenerative, and sustainable systems. Permaculturists apply these ideas in various fields, including agriculture, architecture, community development, and land management. Agricultural permaculture designs are responsible for creating diversified and productive ecosystems modeled after natural patterns. These ecosystems promote the soil's health, water conservation, and overall sustainability. Regarding design, permaculture principles guide the creation of environmentally conscious, energy-efficient structures that mix in with their surroundings. Permaculture is a method of community development that emphasizes local resources, renewable energy, and collaborative techniques. This method helps to cultivate communities that are highly resilient and self-sufficient.

The impact of permaculture extends beyond the scope of individual projects, affecting how civilizations approach the management of resources and the utilization of land. For communities to make the transition from behaviors that are exploitative and degrading to practices that are regenerative and sustainable, they must first embrace the principles of permaculture. This transition is beneficial not only to the environment but also to society and the economy. It helps cultivate a feeling of community, shared responsibility, and resilience in uncertainty.

On the other hand, the widespread implementation of permaculture needs to be improved with difficulties. The prevalence of traditional agriculture practices hampers the integration of permaculture concepts into mainstream systems, land-use policies prioritize short-term advantages over long-term sustainability, and there is a need for more understanding of permaculture principles. There must be a concerted effort in education, advocacy, and policy reform to overcome these challenges. A more widespread paradigm shift toward sustainable and regenerative methods may occur if awareness of permaculture projects continues to rise and communities continue to observe the success of these initiatives.

The principles of permaculture provide a complete and integrative framework for designing systems that are sustainable and regenerative through their use of these principles. Adaptability, efficiency, and plenty are all fostered through permaculture, which is based on the ideas and patterns found in nature. At a time when the world is struggling to find solutions to environmental problems, permaculture shines as a ray of light, revealing that both people and the Earth are capable of living together in harmony. Through careful observation, inventive design, and a dedication to sustainability, permaculture opens the way for a future in which human systems will seamlessly integrate with the natural world, thereby promoting a more robust and vibrant planet.

Off-Grid Gardening Tips

In self-sufficiency and sustainable living, off-grid gardening is a cornerstone practice that enables individuals and communities to cultivate their food independently of conventional utilities. Agriculture that does not rely on external power sources, water infrastructure, or traditional gardening practices is called off-grid gardening. This type of gardening involves growing fruits, vegetables, herbs, and other plants. This section discusses the fundamental ideas and tips for practical off-grid gardening. The study delves into the significance of resourcefulness, water conservation, soil health, and regenerative practices in developing resilient and productive off-grid gardens.

Resourcefulness is one of the most important characteristics to possess in the world of off-grid gardening. It is essential to make the most of the available resources, regardless of whether you are on a rural homestead or a rooftop in the city. The adoption of the concepts of permaculture, which emphasizes resource efficiency and deliberate design, might serve as a guide for off-grid gardeners in making the most of their environment. To accomplish this, it is necessary to observe natural patterns, use recycled materials for garden structures, and incorporate companion planting to increase biodiversity and decrease the requirement for external inputs.

Off-grid gardening, in which access to conventional water sources may be restricted, emphasizes water conservation more than regular gardening. Gathering and storing water for gardening becomes vital when rainwater harvesting is utilized. Gardeners not connected to the grid can harness the power of natural precipitation by installing straightforward rain barrels or more elaborate systems that include filters and distribution pipes. In addition, the selection of drought- resistant plant species and the implementation of effective irrigation methods, like drip irrigation or soaker hoses, help reduce the amount of wasted water and maximize the distribution of moisture throughout the garden.

There is a significant reduction in synthetic fertilizers

and pesticides in off-grid farming, meaning soil health is paramount. The cultivation and upkeep of nutrient-rich soil through mulching, cover cropping, and composting become an absolute necessity. The process of composting organic matter, such as leftovers from the kitchen and garden, not only lessens the requirement for additional inputs from outside sources but also improves the fertility and structure of the soil. Cover cropping entails growing particular crops to protect and enrich the soil during fallow periods. This practice contributes to the control of weeds, nitrogen fixation, and agriculture's overall health. To retain soil moisture, suppress weeds, and regulate soil temperature, mulching, which can be accomplished with materials such as straw or leaves, creates an environment favorable to plant growth.

Regenerative gardening strategies are essential in off-

grid gardening because they emphasize the revitalization and improvement of the natural ecosystems in the areas where gardens are located. Some of the ideas underpinning permaculture, like "observe and interact" and "use and value diversity," are congruent with regenerative methods. Through careful observation and comprehension of the local ecosystem, off-grid gardeners can collaborate with natural processes rather than working against them. Incorporating a wide variety of plant species, creating habitats for beneficial insects, and promoting soil health are all components of regenerative practices that go beyond the concept of sustainability and strive to improve the environment in which they are implemented actively.

Gardeners who operate off the grid frequently confront difficulties in terms of energy supply, particularly in those who live in distant areas that need access to the electrical grid. When circumstances like these arise, it is necessary to prioritize energy-efficient tools and appliances. Using hand tools for gardening tasks such as planting, weeding, and harvesting not only helps conserve energy but also makes gardening a more peaceful and contemplative experience. Gas-powered machinery can be replaced with manual or animal-powered plows and cultivators for bigger plots of land. These options are feasible alternatives. The use of low-tech solutions not only serves to lessen the environmental impact but also helps cultivate a more profound connection to the gardening process.

When contemplating off-grid gardening in regions with more severe temperatures or terrains that present challenges, it is vital to develop new solutions adapted to the particular area. In arid locations, for instance, the implementation of effective water-harvesting systems, such as earthworks or swales, can gather and channel rainwater to the areas where it is required the most. In regions subjected to intense sunshine or strong gusts, it may be necessary to construct windbreaks or shade structures. Possessing adaptability and a desire to experiment with various approaches to achieve success in off-grid gardening in multiple locations is essential.

The concept of off-grid gardening encompasses not just individual plots but also more considerable communal efforts, each of which contributes to the collective resilience of the community through the sharing of resources and knowledge. Examples of initiatives that can cultivate a sense of community and self-sufficiency include rooftop gardens, community gardens, and joint farming endeavors. Off-grid gardening activities are more likely to be successful when they are supported by a network of support created by sharing seeds, tools, and experience. In addition, communal gardens offer chances for education, the exchange of skills, and the celebration of food production in the local area.

To empower individuals and communities to adopt off-grid gardening, educational programs play a critical role in supporting this endeavor. The dissemination of information regarding sustainable and regenerative practices, water-saving measures, and innovative gardening solutions can be accomplished through workshops, internet resources, and community outreach programs. It is possible to promote a sense of autonomy, resilience, and environmental stewardship in individuals by providing them with the technical skills necessary to cultivate their food. Education also debunks myths and misconceptions about off-grid gardening, demonstrating that it is feasible and can bring about positive change.

Devoting to organic and chemical-free farming practices is inextricably linked to off-grid gardening. The concepts of environmental sustainability and human health are aligned with the practice of avoiding the use of synthetic pesticides and fertilizers. On the other hand, off-grid gardeners rely on natural solutions, such as practicing companion planting to ward off pests, attracting beneficial insects, and rotating crops to break the cycle of pests. The cultivation of organic plants not only results in the production of more nutritious and healthier food but also contributes to the preservation of biodiversity and the general well-being of the ecosystem.

Off-grid gardening revolves around cultivating various plant species, which becomes an essential component. Growing a wide range of crops creates a wide range of flavors and nutritional profiles and helps strengthen the ecosystem's biodiversity. Monoculture, which refers to the practice of cultivating a single crop, is more susceptible to the presence of pests and diseases, which necessitates the use of additional inputs to sustain productivity. Polyculture, which involves the intermixing of diverse plant species, is something that off-grid gardeners embrace to build a garden ecology that is balanced and harmonious and lives on diversity.

In conclusion, off-grid gardening is a revolutionary approach to food cultivation that moves beyond the conventional standards of food growing and embraces sustainable, regenerative, and community-oriented methods. Gardeners who operate off the grid can cultivate robust and productive gardens that can flourish without the assistance of conventional utilities. They emphasize water conservation, soil health, and regenerative principles. These gardens not only serve as a source of fresh and nutritious food, but they also contribute to the preservation of the natural world, the development of communities, and a more profound connection to the beauty of the natural world. Off-grid gardening is emerging as a powerful and empowering alternative, offering a route toward a more self-sufficient and harmonious future. This happens when the globe struggles with environmental difficulties and the need for sustainable living practices.

Raising Livestock for Self-Sufficiency

In the pursuit of self-sufficiency and sustainable living, raising livestock is a fundamental practice that has been integral to human societies for centuries. To accomplish this task, appropriate and ethical management of animals for a variety of purposes, including the production of food, fiber, and other critical resources, is required. This section investigates the numerous facets of raising cattle for self-sufficiency. The principles, benefits, and problems of this practice are analyzed, as well as its transforming role in creating resilient and sustainable systems.

When it comes to keeping livestock for self-sufficiency, ethical and humane treatment is one of the primary concepts that guide the activity. One of the most critical aspects of sustainable animal husbandry is the provision of animals with suitable living conditions, the opportunity to engage in natural behaviors, and the utilization of humane treatment throughout their lives. The broader philosophy of self-sufficiency, which emphasizes a harmonious interaction between people and animals, is consistent with this philosophical idea. Providing animals with ethical care ensures that they are well and happy and helps improve the quality of the goods that are ultimately derived from these animals, such as meat, dairy products, or fiber.

One of the most important reasons for raising animals in a self-sufficient lifestyle is to provide food, which stands out as a primary motive. Through the provision of necessary proteins, lipids, and micronutrients, livestock contribute to developing a diverse and nutrient-dense diet. Chickens, goats, pigs, and cattle are frequently raised for food. In the case of chickens, for example, they produce eggs and meat, while goats also offer milk, meat, and fiber. The availability of a wide variety of livestock options enables individuals and communities to adjust their livestock selections to meet the specific dietary requirements and preferences of their populations. Raising animals for food within a self-sufficient framework emphasizes ethical and sustainable practices, eliminating the possibility of overexploitation and guaranteeing the long-term health of both the animals and the land.

The creation of other valuable resources is another way in which livestock contributes to self-sufficiency, in addition to feeding animals. Wool and other natural fibers are acquired from animals that produce fiber, such as sheep and alpacas. These fibers are utilized in the production of textiles and garments. Individuals can lessen their reliance on industrial textiles and partake in the time-honored craft of manufacturing their clothing by incorporating these animals into a self-sufficient system. This technique encourages a connection to historical skills and coincides with ethical fashion and an environmentally responsible fashion industry.

When it comes to self-sufficient farming systems,

manure, which is typically regarded as a waste product, becomes a valuable resource. The nutrient-dense fertilizer that is livestock manure helps to improve the fertility of the soil and encourages the growth of plants that are in good health. The natural recycling of nutrients is made possible by incorporating animals into a rotational grazing system, in which the animals migrate across various parts of the land. One example of a regenerative approach to agriculture is the symbiotic relationship between cattle and the land. This relationship adds nutrients to the soil and reduces the amount of external inputs that are required.

Integrating animals into holistic farm systems is another

fundamental principle that must be adhered to while growing livestock to achieve self-sufficiency. These systems, modeled after natural ecosystems, acknowledge the connectivity between plants, animals, and the surrounding environment. As an illustration, chickens can be incorporated into vegetable gardens to provide pest control, weed management, and fertilizer through their scratching and foraging activities. The employment of goats for targeted grazing is another method that can be utilized to decrease invasive plant species and lower the likelihood of wildfires. Individuals can maximize resource utilization and improve the system's overall resilience by carefully incorporating livestock into more comprehensive agriculture techniques.

However, the endeavor of keeping cattle to achieve self-

sufficiency has its challenges. When it comes to animal husbandry that is both ethical and responsible, it is vital to take into consideration the availability of veterinary treatment, adequate space, and suitable infrastructure. Access to available land or the limits imposed by zoning regulations in urban and suburban regions might be obstacles for individuals who want to raise animals. Additionally, the initial costs of creating infrastructure, such as shelters, fencing, and water systems, might be a barrier for persons interested in embarking on a journey toward self-sufficiency with cattle.

One of the most critical responsibilities regarding self-sufficient livestock management is checking the animals' well-being and ensuring their health. This includes ensuring that the individual receives the proper nutrients, attending to their medical requirements, and establishing living environments that encourage natural activities. It is necessary to incorporate preventative measures, such as vaccination programs and parasite management, to ensure that the animals maintain a high level of overall health. By the principles of sustainable and ethical living, the commitment to animal welfare helps to cultivate a connection with animals that is both balanced and respectful, which in turn contributes to the development of self-sufficiency.

As the concept of sustainable living becomes more prevalent, the environmental impact of livestock farming is becoming an increasingly important issue of discussion. Large-scale industrial livestock operations have been linked to deforestation, emissions of greenhouse gases, and water pollution. This is even though appropriate animal husbandry techniques contribute to the health of ecosystems. Regarding livestock management, the concepts of self-sufficiency emphasize small-scale, regenerative, and holistic approaches that stress ethical treatment and environmental care. Humans can reduce the impact of raising livestock on the environment and contribute to the restoration of ecosystems by using strategies such as rotational grazing, agroforestry, and integrated animal systems.

When it comes to fostering biodiversity and resilience within self-sufficient systems, incorporating heritage or traditional breeds of livestock is a significant factor. Traditional breeds are typically better able to adapt to the environmental circumstances of their respective regions, possess genetic diversity, and may exhibit characteristics that make them more suitable for more environmentally friendly agricultural practices. Individuals contribute to the preservation of genetic resources, resilience in the face of changing climates, and the maintenance of cultural practices associated with specific breeds by supporting the conservation of these breeds.

Community participation and information exchange are also essential elements of effective self-sufficient livestock cultivation techniques. One can gain vital insights and support through participation in local agricultural networks, attendance at workshops, and collaboration with seasoned farmers. Individuals can participate in a cooperative approach to self-sufficiency through community-supported agriculture (CSA) models. These models involve the purchase of shares in a local farm by individuals.

It helps communities become more resilient. Through exchanging information, resources, and experiences, individuals can collaboratively manage the hurdles of keeping livestock to achieve self-sufficiency and enjoy the benefits of doing so.

It is essential to dispel the myths surrounding the practice of keeping livestock to achieve self-sufficiency through education and outreach initiatives. Inspiring and empowering individuals to engage on the road toward self-sufficiency with livestock can be accomplished by promoting awareness of ethical and sustainable methods, displaying successful instances, and giving practical direction. By incorporating agricultural education into school curriculum, community workshops, and internet platforms, a more comprehensive awareness of the connectivity between food production, sustainable living, and ethical animal husbandry can be achieved.

In conclusion, the practice of keeping cattle to achieve self-sufficiency is a transforming activity in accordance with the values of ethical living, environmental stewardship, and resilience. Individuals and communities can include animals in varied farming systems beyond providing nutrition if they cultivate a holistic approach to animal husbandry. The concepts of self-sufficiency in livestock management emphasize the significance of administering ethical treatment, responsibly using resources, and incorporating regenerative farming practices into cattle management. By taking this approach, raising livestock becomes essential to sustainable living, contributing to a more robust and peaceful coexistence between humans, animals, and the land.

CHAPTER VII

Navigating Off-Grid Challenges

Common Obstacles and Solutions

Embarking on any journey, whether personal or professional, is often accompanied by a set of challenges and obstacles that test one's resolve and ingenuity. To shape the route toward success and fulfillment, it is necessary to overcome these obstacles, which are an integral part of growth and achievement. This section investigates the typical challenges encountered in various facets of life and offers insights into practical solutions that can build resilience, adaptability, and a positive outlook.

One of the most common challenges people have when it comes to personal growth is managing their time effectively. It can be challenging to balance one's professional life, family life, and private activities in the fast-paced and linked world we live in. It is possible to find a solution by developing successful habits in managing time. To maximize the use of one's time, it is possible for individuals to prioritize work, establish attainable goals, and break down those goals into more achievable steps. Individuals are given the ability to develop a daily routine that is both purposeful and structured when they make use of various tools and approaches, such as time-blocking, calendars, and to-do lists. Every individual can maximize their productivity and make room for their personal development and fulfillment if they can master time management.

In the business world, disagreements in the workplace can provide considerable obstacles. Whether they are caused by differences in communication styles, competing priorities, or interpersonal dynamics, workplace disputes can impede collaboration and productivity. Effective communication and the resolution of conflicts are the two methods that will be necessary to overcome this challenge. The promotion of communication that is both open and honest helps to cultivate a culture in which problems may be addressed proactively. Individuals and groups can traverse differences constructively when conflict resolution tactics are implemented. Some examples of these strategies include mediation and team-building exercises. By cultivating a culture that emphasizes mutual respect and understanding, businesses can transform disagreements into opportunities for growth and innovation.

Concerns over one's financial situation are a typical issue that many people encounter. The management of spending, the accumulation of savings for the future, and the handling of unforeseen financial setbacks can all be stressful. Financial knowledge and being proactive with one's financial planning are the solutions to this problem. Individuals get the ability to make well-informed judgments regarding their financial situation when they educate themselves on topics such as budgeting, investing techniques, and debt management. Proactive actions toward achieving financial stability include the creation of a budget that is based on reality, the establishment of financial goals, and the creation of an emergency fund. Individuals can further improve their financial literacy and equip themselves with the tools necessary to overcome economic uncertainties by seeking financial experts' assistance and using technology, such as budgeting applications.

Academic challenges can be a substantial source of stress when achieving one's educational objectives. During their educational journey, students frequently come against obstacles, whether they are confronted with challenging assignments, academic pressure, or difficulty managing their availability. Developing productive study habits and reaching out for assistance when required are the solutions to this problem. Enhancing one's comprehension and ability to remember information can be accomplished by establishing a study schedule, dividing complex subjects into more manageable portions, and adopting active learning strategies. Requesting assistance from instructors, tutors, or classmates helps to cultivate an atmosphere that encourages collaborative learning. Additionally, keeping a healthy work-life balance and implementing approaches for stress management, such as mindfulness or exercise, are both factors that contribute to overall academic achievement.

A significant hurdle that arises in interpersonal relationships is a communication breakdown. Interpersonal connections come with their own unique set of problems. Relationships can be put under stress when there are misunderstandings, differences in communication styles, and disputes that are not resolved. Improving one's communication ability and growing empathy are the two critical components of the remedy. Healthy communication is characterized by the following characteristics: active listening, clear expression of oneself, and the selection of reasonable times for discussions. Individuals who have developed their emotional intelligence can comprehend and manage their feelings and those of other people. Through cultivating open and courteous communication, individuals can fortify their relationships, build trust in one another, and negotiate obstacles together.

Within entrepreneurship, business owners frequently face the issue of adjusting their operations to accommodate shifting market conditions. Alterations in the economy, advances in technology, and evolving customer preferences are all factors that might affect a firm's profitability. To find a solution, it is necessary to embrace adaptation and innovation. Companies that have a keen awareness of the trends in the market, make investments in research and development, and maintain a flexible approach to their business strategy are better suited to deal with unpredictability. To encourage employees to contribute to new solutions and adapt to changing conditions, it is essential to cultivate a culture of innovation. Businesses have the power to survive in dynamic and competitive marketplaces and prosper in those markets if they develop a culture of adaptation.

The maintenance of a healthy lifestyle can be a

continuous hurdle when it comes to the field of personal health and well-being. Maintaining a healthy balance between physical activity, diet, and mental well-being demands conscious effort. An approach to health that takes a comprehensive perspective is the answer to the problem. Several factors contribute to general well-being, including making regular physical activity a priority, embracing a balanced diet, and cultivating mental health through activities such as meditation or mindfulness. The likelihood of long-term success can be increased by gradually establishing healthy habits, setting attainable objectives, and obtaining support from health professionals or support groups. The challenge of sustaining a healthy lifestyle can be solved by individuals who adopt the perspective that health is a holistic and ongoing journey.

Navigating societal expectations and cultural

conventions can create one-of-a-kind hurdles, particularly for those looking to forge their path. Being under pressure to conform to the expectations of society can limit creativity and make it more difficult to achieve personal contentment. To find a solution, it is necessary to embrace sincerity and resilience. There is a correlation between those who genuinely articulate their values, beliefs, and objectives and the likelihood that they will build meaningful and rewarding lives. By establishing a support network of persons or mentors who share similar values, one might receive encouragement and direction on the less traveled path. Individuals can construct a life congruent with who they are by cultivating the ability to be resilient in the face of societal expectations.

In conclusion, the ability to overcome challenges is an unavoidable component of the human experience. However, the most critical factor in overcoming obstacles is embracing proactive techniques and focusing on finding solutions. Individuals can utilize successful techniques to handle these obstacles, whether they are dealing with difficulties in time management, conflicts in the job, financial hardships, academic barriers, or personal health concerns. Through cultivating resilience, accepting adaptation, and maintaining a positive mindset, individuals can transform challenges into opportunities for personal development, learning, and success. As one progresses through the journey, it becomes less about merely conquering obstacles and more about developing a more self-sufficient and experienced version of oneself.

Emotional and Psychological Aspects

The human experience is a tapestry woven with myriad emotions and intricate psychological nuances. People's emotional and psychological wellbeing is shaped by various feelings, thoughts, and problems they face while navigating life's complexities. This section delves into the complexities of emotions, resilience, the consequences of stress, and the significance of mental health in promoting a healthy and meaningful life. It also examines the significant influence of emotional and psychological components on human lives.

Emotions are essential to the human experience and are sometimes referred to as the language of the soul. Emotions provide a picture of our existence, from the highs of happiness and love to the lows of sorrow and loss. An essential component of emotional intelligence is acknowledging and accepting the broad spectrum of emotions. People with this talent can better negotiate relationships, speak clearly, and arrive at wise conclusions. Furthermore, being authentic and connected to others and oneself is facilitated by recognizing and expressing positive and negative emotions. The complexity and richness of the human experience are enhanced by the wide range of emotions, underscoring the significance of emotional intelligence and grit in navigating life's path.

It becomes clear that resilience is essential for

overcoming obstacles and uncertainty in life. Resilience is the capacity to overcome hardship; it includes mental, emotional, and even physical toughness. Higher resilient people are typically better able to handle stressors and setbacks, changing with the times and keeping a positive attitude. Developing coping skills, encouraging a growth attitude, and creating a support system are all part of cultivating resilience. People can harness the force of resilience to survive life's storms and come out stronger on the other side by seeing obstacles as chances for progress.

An ever-present companion in life, stress can have a

severe negative effect on one's emotional and psychological health. Chronic stress can have a variety of detrimental consequences on mental health, whether it is caused by demands at work, interpersonal difficulties, or outside events. Stress's physiological effects, such as the production of cortisol and adrenaline, can exacerbate mental health conditions like anxiety and depression. It becomes essential to identify stress symptoms and put efficient stress-reduction techniques into practice to preserve emotional and psychological balance. Stress-reduction strategies, including mindfulness, meditation, and physical activity, have been demonstrated to lessen its effects while enhancing general resilience and mental health.

The complex relationship between the body and mind

emphasizes holistic mental health. Physical health, diet, and exercise directly impact emotional stability and cognitive performance. For example, regular physical activity has been associated with better mood, less anxiety, and increased cognitive performance. In a similar vein, healthy brain function and emotional control are supported by a balanced diet full of vital nutrients. The mind-body connection emphasizes a holistic approach to health, in which mental and physical well-being are seen as interdependent aspects of a harmonious and balanced life.

Whether they are platonic, romantic, or familial, relationships have a significant impact on how people feel emotionally and psychologically. Emotional health, security, and a sense of belonging are all facilitated by helpful and positive connections. Conversely, relationships that are poisonous or tense can negatively affect mental health. Building appropriate boundaries, demonstrating empathy, and having effective communication are essential components of a happy partnership. Emotional resilience and psychological flourishing are enhanced by fostering relationships consistent with one's values and encouraging reciprocal respect. Effective communication, emotional intelligence, and a sincere desire to build healthy connections are all necessary for navigating the intricacies of human relationships.

The search for meaning and purpose in life is closely related to achieving emotional and psychological wellbeing. When people act in a way consistent with their inner principles and further the greater good, they frequently experience intense happiness and fulfillment. This feeling of purpose gives direction in trying circumstances and is a source of resilience and drive. A more profound sense of significance and emotional well-being are brought to life by pursuing purpose through meaningful jobs, creative endeavors, or acts of service. Developing a sense of purpose requires introspection, investigating one's values, and committing to coordinating one's activities with one's highest goals.

Whether it be from a death, a separation, or other life transition, coping with loss is an integral part of being human. A complicated emotional reaction to loss, grief includes a variety of emotions such as sadness, rage, and even relief. Recognizing these feelings and being open to participating in the healing process are essential to navigating grief. Support from friends, family, or licensed counselors can bring comfort and direction during difficult times. In addition, accepting traditions, making tributes to the deceased, and figuring out how to respect their memory all help in the emotional healing process. Even while it might be difficult, grief can also be a transforming experience that leads to acceptance, resiliency, and a greater comprehension of how emotionally mature humans can be.

Frequently disregarded or stigmatized, mental health is essential to general well-being. Mental health illnesses can substantially impact an individual's capacity to lead a satisfying life. These diseases can range from anxiety and depression to more severe conditions. Prioritizing mental health treatment and de-stigmatizing mental health conversations are essential steps in building a society where people feel free to ask for assistance without fear of being judged. Community support, counseling services, and accessible mental health resources are essential for promoting mental wellness. Prioritizing mental health as a crucial element of general health can help people live more resilient, contented, and balanced lives.

The effects of trauma on one's emotional and mental health are severe and long-lasting. Any type of trauma—emotional, psychological, or physical—can have a long-lasting effect on a person's mental health. Healing requires an understanding of the impacts of trauma and the application of trauma-informed therapy practices. Trauma-informed care recognizes the resilience that comes naturally to those who have experienced hardship and emphasizes safety, trust, and empowerment. The emotional and psychological recovery of individuals who have experienced trauma is facilitated by the creation of supportive environments that acknowledge the occurrence of trauma and place a high priority on compassionate care.

Even while it is slowly fading, the stigma associated with mental health issues still poses a significant barrier to general well-being. The widespread misconception that asking for mental health assistance is a sign of weakness or failure frequently discourages people from doing so. To reduce stigma, it is critical to normalize discussions about mental health, support mental health literacy, and include mental health education in school curricula. Societies may create circumstances where people feel empowered, understood, and encouraged to prioritize their mental health by cultivating a culture that views mental health as an essential component of overall wellbeing.

In summary, the psychological and emotional facets of the human experience are complex, multidimensional, and essential to general well-being. A healthy and meaningful existence is facilitated by navigating the intricate web of emotions, developing resilience, controlling stress, and placing a high priority on mental health. The holistic aspect of human health is highlighted by the interaction of connections, purpose, emotional and psychological wellbeing, and the recognition of trauma. A transforming path toward resilience, self-discovery, and a deeper understanding of the human experience can be taken by persons prioritizing mental health as a crucial component of total wellbeing, seeking support when necessary, and cultivating emotional intelligence.

CONCLUSION

In the pages of "Unplugged Living: The Art and Science of Off-Grid Life," readers embark on a transformative journey towards a harmonious and independent existence. The book is both a guide and an intensive investigation of the art and science of off-grid living, highlighting the tremendous beauty and sustainability that this way of life can provide.

The book's title, "Unplugged Living," perfectly sums up its main idea: choosing to live in harmony with nature instead of relying on traditional institutions. The book explores the nuances of living in peace with nature by blending philosophical ideas and practical insights. It reveals the art of sustainable living, stressing the value of permaculture, resourcefulness, and a conscious relationship with the natural environment.

"Creating Harmony with Nature and Independence," the subtitle, sums up the main ideas covered throughout the book. Harmony is more than just living together; it's a profound reverence for the cycles of the natural world and the mutually beneficial interaction between people and their surroundings. In this sense, independence is more than just wanting to be self-sufficient. It represents a deliberate decision to break free from the limitations of mainstream living and to follow a path consistent with resilience, sustainability, and environmental stewardship.

Readers will find much information on anything from off-grid energy options and sustainable agriculture practices to permaculture ideas and water conservation techniques as they progress through the chapters. The e-book is a thorough resource, giving readers the knowledge and skills they need to go off the grid confidently.

"Unplugged Living" is an invitation to rethink life and living environments rather than merely a guidebook. It challenges readers to think critically about accepted wisdom, embrace minimalism, and develop a close bond with nature. By the time the e-book ends, readers will have gained inspiration and confidence to go off the grid and live a life that actively supports the preservation of nature while also honoring its delicate balance.

Thank you for buying and reading/ listening to our book. If you found this book useful/ helpful please take a few minutes and leave a review on the platform where you purchased our book. Your feedback matters greatly to us.